# "IN2 THE MIND OF AN ELEVATING WOMAN"

*"It's not about what they call you but rather about what you answer to."*

*-African Proverb*

*GOLDYN AKACHI*

# GOLDYN AKACHI

*"First, you must learn to ACCEPT, RESPECT, & LOVE yourself for who you really are, before expecting anyone else to give you these things in return."*

*GOLDYN AKACHI*

# CONTENTS

# *THE INTRODUCTION*

Before Eye start this book....Excuse me,.....Before Eye start this conversation with you, Eye just want to let you know that everything that is written, is sincere with honesty and truth. It is also to help encourage you to become as great as you think you can be, because you are. The sky is never the limit but rather the limit is in the mind and as far as you think it is.

You might be wondering why Eye use the word "Eye" instead of "I" and the word "innerstand" rather than the word "understand". You will find the meaning behind it in my other book called "Freedom of the Mind is a Peace of Mind". Until then, you will get the point and message in our upcoming conversations in this book, so don't sweat it or let it get you off track.

Just conversing and walking around just looking at all the different beautiful women and young women, just gives me motivation to inspire as many as Eye can. Nothing is more important in this world to us than our sisters. If they are not right within, then the whole world will be off balanced. Eye have had many conversations with many sisters of all ages and heard some of the most interesting, sad, angry, happy, excited and confused stories of my life that they are experiencing. Sometimes Eye am in amazement and honored that they are willing to open up to me in that way. A sister's sensitivity should be treated like a flower and handled very delicately with caution. Eye also have learned that most of our sisters just want someone to really, really listen to them and hear them. Most sisters want you to really see and innerstand their pain even when they are right or wrong. There is always a root to every problem and a reason for a certain act of character or attitude towards something.

It seems to me that most of our sisters get most of their advice and encouragement from other sisters. Eye just thought that it would be nice for a change for our sisters to start trusting their brothers again to be willing to listen and take in some advice and encouragement from a Man's point of view. Its a saying that says that a Father is always a daughters first love and the first Man she decides to trust. So what happens to that sister when her father was never there or if he decided to hurt her? She will indeed search for that missing void in her life in other Men but not knowing that only her father can fill that void.

Stumbling across Hill Harper's book, "Letters to a Young Sister", inspired me more into writing this book. It seemed that the emails he was getting from sisters were similar to the messages Eye am getting through social media from sisters that are going through certain situations and them just needing some type of encouragement or some kind of advice. Some would just give me their appreciation for just being a listening ear.

He also broke down the meaning of our sisters being so F.I.N.E. Eye am not talking about the sister's body, but rather her mind, when she decides to use it.

F – Fantastic
I – Interesting
N – Necessary
E – Exceptional

An Elevating Woman has the power to change and uplift any Man. She has the power to build or destroy him. Eye have seen it happen so many times to the strongest of Men who say they are not weak over women or would never get into a serious relationship with one. Eye have grew up with some of these famous rappers 2day when Eye use to do music, who use to rap about not loving women and never having kids....but as of now, these same elevating Women have broken them down and made them do all the things they said they wouldn't do.

A Man only pretends that he is so strong and powerful when he wants to attract a female. He is called the cowardly Lion.....Yes, he is strong but he is very unbalanced.... and when that elevating woman approaches, the ground will shake beneath his feet. Then on that day when he decides to uplift his Queen unto her throne beside him, he will become balanced & he will be at his full strength & the two will become a powerful force.

The most important thing in a woman's life is to know who she really is and the power she really has to define her own destiny. Without the woman, there is no us....there is no life. So she should never feel like she is worthless or doesn't have a purpose in this world when she is "Mother Earth".

*"The greatness of a nation is judged by the morals & strength of its women."*

## *"Let Me Be Your Peace of Mind"*

*My sister...look at me....No, close your eyes and really look at me. Feel my energy until you actually see me with your two eyes closed, and your third eye (mind) open. Don't be afraid because Eye am already in tuned with your vibration. Comfort yourself and exhale. Trust me like you trust yourself. Eye know what hurts you and Eye know what is empty inside of you. Why are you holding back this anger and bitterness inside of your heart? Release it now and tell me what's wrong without saying a word to me. Just breathe...just breathe....inhale until your heart starts to fill whole and it starts to beat rapidly. Exhale....take deep breaths like you have just climax. Continue to look at me...Do you see me? Grab my hand without touching me and follow me into calm waters without walking. Let me see you naked, not the physical, but the mental. Come into the water slowly and just ease down until the water covers you. Amazingly the water stops at the top of your chin. That means whatever your body has gone through, can be washed away, cleaned and healed.....but your head cannot be just be covered with water for it to be renewed. It takes you....yes you, it takes you. Close your windows (eyes) and your door (mouth) of your soul and travel within your mind to break all these chains of terrible and negative thoughts that's eating you inside. That's where you find the God within.*

*Once you control your mind, then you control your body. If your mind is broken then your body will be broken as well. Do you feel the calm water on your body? Eye know you do...but that is really the feeling that your mind feels and your body is still dry. So your mind is really the calm water that is really healing your body and all you had to do was to let me be a "peace in your mind".*

*Look at me, Eye mean really look at me and come back to the physical. What if Eye told you that you had your two eyes open the whole time while we were staring eye to eye looking into each other souls? Now, Eye want you to Love and let others love you again like you know how.*

**GOLDYN AKACHI**

4

CHAPTER 1
# "THE CONVERSATION"

*"No person is your friend who demands your silence, or denies your right to grow." -Alice Walker*

Excuse me, my beautiful sister....or should Eye say "my Queen?" Let me talk to you for a minute if you don't mind. Eye know you are so use to different guys approaching you by telling how pretty or sexy you are, but Eye am coming to you at a different angle. Don't believe the rumors or the stereo type that a boy or man cannot approach a woman or girl or be friends with a them without wanting something from her....even though that happens a lot, that is not realistic for all men. A man will always show you who he really is, eventually. All you have to do is pay close attention.

Anyway, how are you doing? How has life been treating you or how have you been treating life? Things can get stressful at times by following the world and it's every move, so Eye hope that you are not a follower. Sometimes it is good and healthy for you to have some kind of alone time. That's where you will always find your peace of mind and your true self when you know no one is watching. In Today's society there is a lot of things going on, especially trends and being about a certain life. Don't get too caught up in the hype, its only temporary and seasonal. Life can get tough sometimes, and it will....and it's okay to cry it out at times because you don't want it to build all up inside and you become this bitter, angry monster. You know the type of women that you see that's always growling and bickering and nagging about everything. Sometimes our mothers can get that way because they have to be strong for the family. We be like, "Okay Mama, Eye heard you, dang."...lol. It's all good though, she means well.....at least sometimes.... Things like that only makes us learn and become stronger individuals.

Growing up as a teen woman Eye hope your not just thinking about the latest fashion or boys. Not saying that there's anything wrong with that, just make sure that is not the only thing that you are spending your time thinking about. It's great to have some kind of hobbies on the side that doesn't concern that. That way you can balance everything out and life would be less stressful. Learn to impress yourself first before you go out your way to impress others. It's so much things to do to be in a position where you are just bored to death. Being bored will sometimes lead you to do things that you don't need to be doing and you will end up regretting them later.

Eye hope this conversation & book is not weird for you or make you feel uncomfortable in any kind of way. Eye don't know the kind of relationship you had in the past with males. Just don't put me in that category of another Man disappointing you or hurting you. Eye am still here and Eye want to innerstand you a little better and try to open your mind up as well as encouraging and uplifting you. You may even feel that no one even takes the time out to listen to how you feel anymore and no one innerstands you, and that's fine. But trust me, you will never know for sure unless you open up to someone. What do you have to loose?

Eye want to ask you a question. Do you dream?
It is so good to dream or have goals or visions of where you want to go or be in life. This is the only way to just get away -mentally- from what's going on at the moment. Sometimes Eye visualize myself at all kinds of beautiful places that Eye will love to go visit. You can even dream big about your future career or husband. Eye know every woman has that one ideal man that they want to see themselves with. Am Eye right?

Our thoughts and dreams are very powerful and we have the

ability to turn our dreams into a reality. All we have to do is to never doubt ourselves, and continue to work hard for what we desire to have. There is no time limit for turning dreams into realities. Always keep that in mind along your journey.

On social media, Eye get a lot of messages through social media when Eye am connecting with females of all ages. Eye learned that no matter the age, race or culture of the woman, they all tend to go through the same struggles in life dealing with self issues or just life itself. Eye won't share them all with you, just a few so you can get an idea of what Eye am talking about. Eye also cropped out the names and picture icons of the women.

It was something that Eye sense going on with this particular woman and Eye asked her what was bothering her. Her Response:

> Unsure of myself. Of my drive. Of my heart. It's deeper than it sounds. I want to achieve my goals but mostly wanna reach my highest self. I wanna raise my children to the best of my abilities to know & be all they could ever dream to be. All they are destined to be. I know I'm capable of it all but will I push myself to do it all is what I question a lot. My mother passed in a car wreck when I was 7 & my dad says after that, every project that I started, I never finished or had a hard time finishing. I'm still getting to know & understand who I really am. So if I'm unsure of anything, it's the uncertainty of whether or not I'll conquer my fears... my doubts. My mind & my heart.

Eye am sure there are other females who feel like her but are too afraid to open up to anyone to talk about these things. We have talked and she is steady growing an elevating to become the woman she is set out to be.

The next message is a touchy subject that Eye will speak on later in this book and how to deal with a situation like that. Believe it or not but a lot of females are going through this as well. Some are probably going through this at the moment and too afraid to say anything. She messaged me this:

> You are pretty knowledgeable and I need to know what should i do. I see you once did a post on sexual abuse in the black home, and you said one of the outcomes of it was a woman can eventually want sex all the time. I was molested when i was younger and now it seems like i am addicted to sex. Like i have to have it almost everyday. I try to fight against it but nothing works. What should i do.?

This message from this female is just informing me on one of her bad days. Something that we all go through. She messaged:

> Hello King,
> Today was a ROUGH day for me today and for a moment well several I was physically upset to the point of tears however, I pulled it together. What I am trying to say is thank you for your words. I just read your last post and I feel like it was for ME!

> Its okay Love...everything is stepping stones...we all hurt sometimes and it's very good to cry it out...release that bad energy....what's bothering you?

Okay, this will be the last one Eye share with you. This is just one of the many messages Eye receive from random females, just telling me that they appreciate my words of wisdom and encouragement. Even though Eye do have others that tend to hate me for whatever reason...people like her keeps me motivated.

> Don't worry about the negative energy. You are a kind selfless and loving. Words are powerful and your words and thoughts have changed many life your book is going to save life. This might sound strange to you but I have love for you and your family then those that I come in contact with each day. Your positive energy has changed my life. Each day I check your FB page to learn something new. I

The reason why Eye shared this with you is to show you proof that a male & female can have a connection or friendship without wanting anything from one another. We have to be there for each other at times because somethings that we go through might consist of us wanting a different advice or opinion from the opposite sex. We have to stop competing with one another and start cooperating with one another. Women are very powerful in their own way and some things that women can do, the men can't. So a woman shouldn't focus more on trying to do everything a Man does. Your biggest mistake is to think that you are not powerful enough. Your struggles bring strength.

Have you ever met someone and you felt a good vibe around them or you couldn't stop staring at them? If so, that is a powerful connection and maybe that person could be a good friend or just someone you can just associate with. Some guys are like that. They just need a female to talk to when they are uncomfortable telling their friends certain things. Some females fight this connection just because its a male or they try to force a connection when there is no connection there. They are only attracted to the way he looks. Never try to associate with everyone because a lot of people carry bad vibes and negative energies. In other words, they bring drama. Building a better you requires you to destroy relationships with some people that is really bad for you that will effect your growth in life. Know the difference between being down for someone rather than being stupid for someone just because you like them.

As a young teen woman or young lady there will be a lot of mistakes that you will make, but you can try to avoid some of them by just listening and paying attention to the warning signs that are given to you by those who have went down that same road. As being young, we all think they we have everything figured out and everything is just fun and games. We laugh at everything and don't have a care in the world....well at least we pretend to not care. One thing you must innerstand and always keep in mind is that you will have to face the consequences of every decision that you decide to make, good or bad. Everything feels right and good while your doing it, but when its over, that's when we start to have doubts about it. We tend to ask ourselves, "Why did Eye do that, What the hell was Eye thinking? Some girls don't have older brothers or fathers to look after them or give them advice from a Man's point of view. A Man is always a Woman's protector, regardless of the age. It's good to have that sisterhood going on but it's even better when you have that sister and brotherhood going on as well.

In your life, you are going to have a lot of goals and dreams. They will continue to switch up a lot as you get older. To not confuse or stress yourself out, just practice on being better than what you were yesterday. You are already a special and unique person, and let me add by saying your beautiful as well....some women just haven"t realized it yet because their focus is caught up into the outer world. There is a shift happening in your life and we have connected through this book for a reason. This means that you want answers. You may feel alone but just remember that there is always someone out there that will take the time out to hear you if their given the chance. Eye may not have all the answers but Eye do innerstand a woman's worth and how much value she has in this world. The time is now for women to pick their heads up and become magic....because that is what you all are...A Magical Rose that can grow from anything and anywhere you are planted in!

*CHAPTER 2*
# "BEING AN ORIGINAL & LOVING YOURSELF"

*"People often say that "beauty is in the eye of the beholder,"and I say that the most liberating thing about beauty is realizing that you are the beholder. This empowers us to find beauty in places where others have not dared to look, including inside ourselves."*
*-Salma Hayek*

My sister, Eye know the world will have you thinking that true beauty is whatever they show you on television or whatever latest trend is out. Let me be the first to tell you if you don't already know.... "That is not true beauty, that is a product and image to sale." Let me ask you this question. What do you define as true beauty or being beautiful?

Let me help you with that question. True beauty is when you finally accept how you was created as you look at your reflection in the mirror. It's when you embrace every single detail about you....even if you think that you have flaws, love and embrace those as well. Sometimes it's okay to decorate yourself with a little makeup but before you do that, make sure you love what's under that makeup first. Believe it or not but there are so many women and young teen girls who think they are so ugly without makeup. That is a bold lie and Eye do not want you to ever think that you are ugly.

What really is the definition of being physically ugly? Is ugly being defined of what is not popular to our peers or friends? Just because you don't look like the people that you think are pretty or beautiful, doesn't mean that you fit the ugly category. Don't worry about those foolish, immature boys who chooses what the false, popular definition of beauty is. Boys and Men will only go for what is tempting and popular to have. It's like they are following a trend as well. They want the video, model, stripper girls...lol. So please don't belittle your true beauty just to get them to notice you. Sometimes the grass is more beautiful on the other side because it is fake.

"Beauty should not be dictated, but should instead be an expression of a woman's freedom to be herself." – **Lupita Nyong'o**

There was this beautiful girl that was a freshman in highschool and she was the type where she just wanted to be accepted or wanted to just fit in with the popular girls. So every chance she got, she tried to make herself look like the girls that she wanted to hang around. She cut her hair, cut her eyebrows, changed her wardrobe, change the way she walked and changed the way she talked, just to be just like the others. To make a long story short, she was stressing herself out so much trying to keep up that she eventually ended up loosing her true identity. She didn't even know who she was anymore. No matter how often you stay out with the crowd, you will have to always go home alone to face yourself in the mirror to look and to deal with your true self. If you are not happy within, it is impossible to be happy without.

Why settle to be a follower when you are meant to be an original and a leader. Maybe it was meant to you to inspire someone else to embrace their own beauty, because we are all beautiful in our own way. Look around, Eye know sometimes we may wonder how some of these girls that we might not find attractive, are in love relationships with descent looking people. You see, someone was attracted to their true original beauty. A real Man or boy sometimes doesn't want a carbon copy, but rather he wants the original. If everyone is meant to look the same, then we will all act the same. Eye don't know about you but that is a boring world to be caught up in.

Truly loving yourself can be difficult sometimes, especially when you expect perfection from yourself or when you continuously fail at something. Being perfect is not about just doing things right. Being perfect is knowing that you are putting your all into whatever you decide to do. It's about knowing that you didn't let yourself down and the others around you that loves you. If you can look yourself in the mirror and honestly tell yourself that you did the best you can, then you are perfect. That's how you fall in love with yourself. Even if you decide you want to be better, you have to love yourself even more to elevate. When really loving yourself it is best for you to not put yourself in a position in life where someone is hurting you and influencing you to become a horrible person.

Don't be afraid to fail, because you will at times. Accept yourself, love yourself and keep moving forward. If you want to fly, you have to give up the weight that's holding you down. Also you have to forgive yourself as well as being true to yourself. How you treat yourself sets the standard for how others will treat you. Please learn to encourage yourself when you are not getting it enough from other people. Love has no doubts....so never doubt yourself. It was a time that many girls doubted themselves....even women. They have passed up many opportunities and people that came into their lives that was meant to stay, but they couldn't hold on to them or accept those opportunities because they didn't love themselves. They doubted and didn't trust their intuition. It's hard to feel desire when you don't feel desirable. Even in your loneliest moments, you have to be there for yourself. Those who mistrust their own abilities are being too wicked to themselves, discouraging themselves from doing what they should have been excelling in. Once you get good at encouraging yourself, you can become a great leader because leadership is built on inspiring others to face challenges.

Whatever you decide to do, be gentle with yourself. You don't just live in this world....You just don't live in your home or your skin....You also live in someone's eyes. Eventually we will learn that in this life the "other self" is more powerful than the physical self that we see in the mirror. Meaning, what ever you feel inside is what defines you. Love yourself a little bit longer, until you can't stand not to love someone else. It is okay to be a quiet person and to not want to be around people all the times, Eye innerstand that. That doesn't mean that you don't love yourself, that is just your personality. Your creator doesn't make mistakes....your are just at a growing stage of getting to know yourself a little better.

Learning to love yourself is like learning to walk. You will go through so many life changes that will make you have no choice but to stand tall. Loving yourself isn't about celebrating your accomplishments and flaunting your talents. Those things are nice and all, but that's not how we know others love us. We know others love us when they see us with our face on the ground, crying and weak, feeling like we have nothing to offer the world....and they smile, and they reach out, and they love us anyway. Loving yourself is what you do when you fail, when you don't know, when you screw up, when you forget, when you loose everything. Loving yourself is what you do when you can't approve of what you have done. Loving yourself is what you do when your not sure if it's going to get better. Loving yourself is what you must do in those moments when you can't like yourself. Real love is when you reach out for no good reason at all, except to love.

Recently Eye had a conversation with this 21 year old woman and we came up with this conclusion on loving herself:

"As Eye began to love myself, Eye found out that my emotional suffering were only warning signs that Eye was living against my own truth."

"As Eye began to love myself, Eye innerstood how much it can offend somebody if Eye try to force my desires on this person, even though Eye knew the time was not right and the person was not ready for it. Eye call that ***Respect***."

"As Eye began to love myself, Eye stopped craving for a different life, and Eye could see that everything that surrounded me was inviting me to grow. Eye called that *Maturity*."

"As Eye began to love myself, Eye innerstood that at any circumstance, Eye am in the right place at the right time, and everything happens at the exact moment. So Eye should remain calm. Eye call that ***Self-Confidence***".

"As Eye began to love myself, Eye quit stealing my own time, and Eye stopped designing huge projects for the future. Today, Eye only do what brings me joy and happiness, things Eye love to do and that makes my heart cheer, and Eye do them in my own way and in my own rhythm. Today Eye call it ***Simplicity***."

"As Eye began to love myself, Eye freed myself of anything that is no good for my health......- food, people, things, situations, and everything that drew me down and away from myself. At first Eye called this a healthy attitude but Today eye call it ***Love of Oneself***."

"As Eye began to love myself, Eye quit trying to always be right, and ever since Eye was wrong less of the time. Today Eye call it ***Modesty***."

"As Eye began to love myself, Eye refused to go on living in the past and worrying about the future. Now, Eye only live for the moment, where everything is happening. Today Eye live for each day, day by day, and Eye call it **Fulfillment**."

"As Eye began to love myself, Eye recognized that my mind can disturb me and it can make me sick. But as Eye connected it to my heart, my mind became a valuable ally. Today Eye call this connection **Wisdom of the Heart**."

We are no longer need to fear arguments, confrontations or any kind of problems with ourselves or others. Even stars collide, and out of their crashing, new worlds are born. Today Eye know that is called **"Life"**.

*"Be an original"*

If you learn to really sit with loneliness and embrace it for the gift that it is.....an opportunity to get to know YOU.....to learn how strong you really are....to depend on no one but YOU for your happiness....you will then realize that a little loneliness goes along way in creating a richer, deeper, more vibrant and colorful YOU.

One of the greatest regrets that you will ever have in your life is being what others would want you to be. If you celebrate your differences and your originality, the world will too. It believes exact;y what you tell it.....through the words you use to describe yourself, the actions you take to care for yourself, and the choices you make to express yourself. Tell the world you are one-of-a-kind creation who came here to experience wonder and spread joy. Expect to be accommodated.

There is a magnificent, beautiful, wonderful painting in front of you. It is very detailed, a labor of devotion and love. The colors are like no other, they swim and leap, they trickle and embellish. And yet you choose to fix and focus your eyes on the small fly which has landed on it. Why do such a thing when there is no beauty like yourself?

*Chapter 3*
# "A DAUGHTER'S FIRST LOVE"

***"I know that I will never find my father in any other man who comes into my life because it is a void that can be filled by him."***
***-Halle Berry***

The relationship between a daughter and her father is so pure and she grows into a woman from that relationship. This relationship sometimes determines what she thinks of a man. Having a real father in a young girl's life will teach her the meaning of security, patience, unconditional love, loyalty, comfort, and respect....and so much more.

As that elevating woman grows up with her father, she watches his every move on how he treats women, especially her mother, if she's in the home. If her mom is happy, so is the daughter. She learns balance. Eye don't know what it is but most women say that it is a special kind of bond that they have with their father that they cannot explain. It's like a fulfillment inside that keeps them from being angry all the time. Eye guess that every woman needs at least one man that they can trust and count on.

Like most girls, a father is her first love. She adores everything about him, even how he smells and the scent of his clothes. The sound of his voice will make her heart skip a beat. The demanding and conquering approach that he has at times, knowing that she is safe. All she want to be is daddy's girl. She values her father's opinion even if it's not what she wants to hear......it's just knowing that he actually cares and takes time out just to listen to her. This calms her down and soothes her worries. If a young woman gets that affirmation and approval from her father, she is not going to be desperate to get it anywhere else because she already has it in him. Real Fathers teaches young women that you can be happy on your own without a man and that you are enough by yourselves at the moment. Eye am not saying that you don't need a man....Eye am saying that you will learn that you don't need to rush into dating or marrying someone to feel complete for the moment when you are trying to fulfill that emptiness that you feel inside from the lack of love.

Sometimes a little girl or woman will just hug her father and she can just feel the love without him saying a word, A real father will always be that shoulder that you can lean on.

A daughter thinks her father is the smartest, best looking, and best-smelling man she knows. One day she will look for a mate that she will most likely compare every young man to him. As the father being that woman's first love, he sets the bar for her future relationships with men.

**Building a relationship with your father:**

You might be wondering or asking me how do Eye build a relationship with my father? If you notice in the beginning of this chapter Eye have been giving you the definition of a REAL father and how he makes his daughter feel. Believe it or not, some men do not know how to be fathers or how to build that connection or relationship with their daughters. So you might have to make the first move and to just open up to him and tell him how you feel. This relationship is so important to have because it will effect your life forever, so its worth the effort. Also you cannot forced the situation or make someone give you that love when they don't want to. So that's why Eye mentioned before that you have to tell him how you feel and that you want that relationship with him. If he decides that he wants that relationship with you then that's when you proceed.

Be open with him. Learn to feel comfortable telling him about anything. You have to first build up that trust with him by knowing that you can count on him for just simple things like taking where you need to go or fulfilling his promises that he have made to you on other things. Be open with him about boys/men, sex, etc,etc. Try to schedule daddy/daughter dates where it's just you guys going out just to hang together while talking or just to have fun. Whenever you are hurting or feeling sad or stressed out about something, don't be afraid to open up to him so he could comfort you. No man likes to see his daughter hurting if he actually loves and cares for her.

It's really about just being honest and open with him. Having your father around and having that strong relationship really benefits your dating because your father is a man and he can tell if some boys or other men are no good for you. He may not be right all the times but you will always be aware and will always have your eyes open. So if you want that relationship with your father, just swallow your pride and reach out to him. If you just sit back and say nothing, how would he even know that you actually care to have that relationship with him. Us men are stubborn at times when we get too caught up in the world....so be patient with us, please.

*"Having a father in the home while not having a relationship with him, is worst than not knowing or having a father at all."*

**The effects of not having a father & How to deal with that issue?**

It seems that girls with present and affectionate fathers are less likely to develop eating disorders, behavioral problems, and become depressed more. Of course not all fathers are affectionate, and some are over critical, which robs their daughters of the fatherly affirmation they need. But overall, growing up without a father in the home or not knowing your father is a major risk of depression in teen girls that will cause them to be off balanced emotionally.

This one woman told me that her father's absence left a huge void in her heart, and she went searching for something to fill it, especially when it came to dating. She often settled for less, mostly seeing guys who gave her just enough attention to keep her wanting to stay around. She had difficulty trusting, and she stayed too long in unhealthy relationships. Because she was too afraid to let go to be left alone again. She said when the relationship finally ended, she fell apart.

In fact, most of her depression came from the ending of her many relationships. She told me that when her ex broke up with her or hen she ended the relationship for whatever reason, she experienced the same kind of panic she felt as a child saying goodbye to her dad. This was the first time she began to connect "missing my father" to how she related to other men.

Father's opinions matters to the daughters while growing up. If your mother is single and was neglected by her father then her poor choices in men that she allow in her life will influence you in a negative way. You will struggle with body image issues as well.

There's a saying out there that says that "A hungry person makes the worst shopper and that person will come home with nothing but junk, fast food." Likewise, a father-hungry young woman will go to the dating supermarket and often come home with the worst men.

Young teenage girls who are fatherless tend to be more sexually active than others. They get curious of a man's touch and doesn't innerstand what real love is. They get attached to that sexual feeling that they think is comfort but really, its only lust. It's like an addiction that comes over them that they can't control. It's all in their mind. They are only seeking to be loved by the opposite sex. They convince themselves that the only way they can get a man to truly love them is to give them their bodies and to have their way with them.

If this cycle continue to happens, the female will get weary and depressed again by allowing herself to be apart of the same routines with multiple men. All of her relationships tend to fail and she starts to realize that all these men want is sex. Then she gets bitter and she starts to hate men. She gets curious of the opposite sex and start socializing with other fatherless women. She thinks that if she unite or start dating other women who is broken like her than this will fulfill her empty void inside of her. Wrong, this only makes the cut deeper and the pain worst.

Eye see a lot of fatherless girls walking around are confused as ever. It's like some of you are so timid and uncomfortable when a boy or man speaks to you. You are so insecure that you think every man is out to hurt you or he if wants something from you. Trust me, Eye don't blame you or do Eye hold that against you, Eye innerstand. Sometimes Eye can hug a female and can feel all her broken pieces r=trying to come together. When girls/women give boys/men side hugs, that means that they do not trust them. They are very cautious and aware of being hurt again. You can tell when a real father is in a female's life because she will know how to interact with boys/men. She will give you eye contact and will have some kind of respect for the opposite sex. She will not feel uncomfortable around any man because she have raised her confidence up by having a strong father at home.

Dealing with this issue can be very hard when you are in denial and you have made it up in your mind that you don't need any kind of male guidance in your life. So, in order to deal with this issue and to heal from this situation, you must admit to not having father in your life is affecting you in a negative way. Then you must educate yourself about the impact of not having that father-daughter relationship. Just think about how you tried to fulfill those needs and how you tried to hide that pain. Once you recognize and admit to that, your eyes will start to open up and you will finally be aware of what you are doing.

You have to fight against unhealthy and uncivilized behaviors that are damaging your relationships with people, especially the opposite sex. Just because you are meant to act like this doesn't mean that you have to act on it. You still have your free-will to choose how you want to carry yourself. You may be wondering why you are drawn to no good men are men that you know you can't have. You must resist that temptation knowing that you are only attracted to the attention of that male.

Also you have to analyze and pay attention to other men. You must reach out to father-like men. This could be an uncle, brother, friend, etc,etc....Once you have educated yourself on what a real father should be like then you will not a a problem on meeting these type of father figures. Don't be afraid to share your hurt and weaknesses with your boyfriend or husband and make sure you ask for his helping hand, his patience as you try to overcome the past.

Father-hunger issues can give you a deeper appreciation for the role that father's play in their children lives. You can meet guys or relatives or even the guy that you are with interact with his daughter and know that she is not missing those special moments with him that will shape her life. Seeing this really helps heals you because you will know that real father's still exist and you won't be as bitter to have this hate in your heart about men. What matters the most is that these other girls will not spend their lives aching for her first love and trying to fill that father-sized hole in their hearts with anything else.

Even though it's hard but you must put away the hurtful emotions you feel within your heart and start focusing with your mind and what you need to do to move forward. You cannot keep carrying this burden and baggage with you, so you must let this situation make you a stronger person. Make your long-lost father regret for ever leaving you or if he passed away, make him proud.

To overcome this, do not keep bring attention to your pain, but rather keep going forward and to help others rather than yourself. Isolating yourself will not help you heal but rather it will multiply your pain. Eye encourage you to share both publicly and privately by meeting with fatherless daughters where they are too overcoming this.

*Chapter 4*
# "CHARACTER, MORALS & SELF-CONTROL"

*"It's not the load that breaks you down, it's the way you carry it."*
*-Lena Horne*

**Character:**

You may ask me, "What is character".....well character is basically how you carry yourself in a mental way that involves you when you are put in different situations. This is something that you create and build up as you go through life. You and only you must be responsible for the character you decide to build up or create.

The message Eye am giving you is to **NOT** choose to have a bad character. There are several things to evaluate yourself on if you have bad character. One is.... if you find yourself speaking bad about others all the time. If you do this you will eventually find something wrong with everyone you meet. To break this and to create a good character you must focus more on the positive things about the people you interact or communicate with. Others will see it and positive people will be drawn to you.

Be on the lookout to see how you treat others. For example, if you are out in public like a restaurant, or shopping store, evaluate on how you treat the employees, waiters or waitresses. Are you being abusive or innerstanding of people? Kindness is free, so there is no excuse to be an asshole.

Building character consist of your top values in life, and you have to be specific. If you focus on things that are purely superficial, like fame and wealth, chances are that you won't stick it out through the rough patches in life with anyone when your in a relationship with anyone. On the flip side, if you value loyalty, honesty, trust, and health, chances are you will appreciate a good person who treats you well. Eye know you hear other girls talking and acting as if they are already a celebrity or to good or stuck up to socialize with anyone with dreams of not being a popular person. That is the definition of bad character.

As you build your character it is so much easier to be around others who have good character. To see what kind of character they have you must behave in a casual relaxed manner. This is important, because in order to get people to reveal their true character, it's essential that you don't make them feel judged for being themselves. So try to be as relaxed as possible when interacting with someone. Asking them about their values must be done in a way where they do not feel like there is a right or wrong answer. Don't come across as being too serious, or they will only present to you their "formal" self which is more of an act, rather than who they really are naturally.

A woman with good character is the kind of person who is able to apologize and own up to making a mistake. If you are not able to do this, you will be a horrible person to have a relationship with, for your ego is so big that you can't admit your mistakes or learn from them. There are a lot of sisters out there who just put the blame on everyone but themselves like they do no wrong. Please don't be one of those people.

Eye know this is a question that will make you think hard about yourself. How do you behave when you are under stress? If you are still behaving in a way that is kind, honest, respectable and sensitive, then you are growing into become an amazing woman. However, if you are always spiteful, hateful, or abusive, this is an indicator of how you will be in the future when under any type of stress. And life definitely will have its stressful moments, so you can be sure such a woman will behave badly again in the future. Don't be easily provoked by people because they will try you all the time. Their mission is to make you come out of character and to become low just like them. You have to stand your ground and walk away. Never entertain foolishness even though it may get interesting and entertaining sometimes. If they are not putting their hands on you, then don't worry about it and don't let them make you mad enough to put your hands on them first.

Be very carefully when you speak, because most people give away their personalities very quickly without realizing it. This is because most people don't consciously try to behave badly, so they all think they are great even if in fact they are abusive or cruel.

**Morals:**

Okay, having great morals can be kind of difficult to have if you wasn't taught this growing up as a child. So to build this back up you must start from scratch. This will even work for the women who are in the process of teaching their daughters great morals to have.

First we must learn the important rule and morality of **RESPECT** because One of the most important values to teach yourself or your children is respect. Of all the girls/women that I've seen and hung around had no respect for authority at all. At least some of them. By teaching yourself and your kids respect, you are doing the world, yourself, and your child a favor! Life will go much easier for them with a little respect under their hat. Having respect for yourself and others will stop you from doing or saying negative things negative to others who are different from you. Just like you want someone to respect you as a lady and your opinion on things, you will have to return the favor, don't you think? Also if you believe in something pure or have some kind of religious beliefs, it is good for you to have the respect and morality to do the good things that it tells you to do and the bad things it tells you not to do. That's having respect for what you believe in.

Now lets talk about **OBEDIENCE.** Obedience is something that doesn't come naturally, for any of us! It seems more "fun" to want to break the rules, doesn't it? Kids see it this way too, so you must be firm and consistent. And be patient, sometimes this one takes a while to catch on! Being a young lady or whatever how old you are, Eye am not talking about being obedient to a man like a puppy. Eye am really talking about being obedient to yourself to do what's right regardless of how it makes you feel. Being obedient is sticking to something that you have planned out for yourself, like accomplishing a goal or building yourself to be a certain type of person. Also if you tell someone that you are going to do a particular thing, having obedience within yourself will allow you to do that. Having poor morals will allow you to break your own obedience to yourself and others.

Don't get to a point where you think you can get away with anything just because your a female because life doesn't work that way. You may get away with it a few times but when karma comes back to bite you, it will hurt ten times worst when you are still obedient.

**POLITENESS**....is something that every girl/woman should have within herself. Never let anyone take that away from you. Remembering to say "please" and "thank you" isn't a difficult task, but if kids are never taught or reminded, they will never do it. As adults, we all know that sugar attracts more flies than vinegar! So start teaching these morals from the start and they will come naturally. Being polite to someone will cause them to return the favor and you will absorb this positive, great feeling inside. Some people just choose to be ugly and mean for whatever reason, it's like they don't mind giving up their morals. Just don't let these people change you. A beautiful rose can blossom and grow from any circumstance or garden, remember that.

Believe it or not, children can be taught **RESPONSIBILTY** from a young age! You don't need to be overbearing about it, but giving yourself or your kids easy chores to do, like picking up their toys, putting away their clean laundry, or helping clear the table helps instill discipline and responsibility, two traits that will be helpful later on in life. Another way to teach responsibility is to make sure your kids brush their teeth or do their homework without being reminded.

As for the older women, you will need to build up your responsibility by doing what you have to do as a woman. If you are in school, be responsible to get your school work done and build up your GPA to get into a good college if you are planning to go. Be responsible enough to know that there is a time to play around and a time to be serious and to get things done that you need to get done. As you get older make sure you are paying your bills and getting more things that you actually need rather than spending all your time getting things that you only want for the moment.

Good **MANNERS** may not necessarily be a moral value per se, but you will find that for the most part, good manners are sorely lacking in the young girls of today's generation. It's not always because the parent doesn't teach the child, sometimes it can be due to other kids at school or their own peers who have an influence on them. Make sure to set a good example for manners at home and try to push through any influences that may be overshadowing your small one's life and yours.

We've all heard it said, "**HONESTY** is the best policy." It's as true today as it ever was! If you teach your children honesty from a small age, you won't need to worry about it as they get older. One struggle that parents face is wondering how to deal with a child that will not tell the truth. If you start teaching honesty as a moral value right away, you will have no need to worry about it!

As women, you need to be very honest in every situation, especially concerning the guys you start to date. If you don't like something and if something is bothering you, say something. Don't get to a point where you are making yourself suffer over something that you are holding in. Lying to yourself all the time is very dangerous and unhealthy for you.

**Self-control:**

Lets now talk about self-control because this is another big issue that needs dealing with. This will have a huge effect on your life day in and day out. Eye know you are getting older where you feel that you can just say whatever you want and that no one can tell you anything because you are grown right? That's all fine and dandy and Eye agree to a certain extent. What you fail to realize is that is some things are better left unsaid. Sometimes you have to hold on to your peace of mind so you won't end up doing nothing crazy. Especially in school, your peers will pressure you into doing anything because you all share the same way of thinking and are curious about any and everything. So you must keep some kind of self-control even when those things get tempting to do.

Eye don't know why most girls like to fight at school, it is not lady like at all. Never decide to fight over a boy or just because of some "he say, she say" nonsense. Do you defend yourself is someone hits you first....yes...but always try to find a better solution so you won't get in trouble and to put yourself in a situation that you really do not want to be in. Sometimes you have to just let people talk, because that's only what they are good at. A lot of times you are going to **WANT** to really knock someone out or give them a peace of your mind, but in your mind you know that you don't really **NEED** to lower your standards to do that.

A lot of problems Eye see in young girls were due to a simple lack of self control. They would cave in to peer pressure by boys and girls, and sometimes cave into their own wants, and as a result, they have to suffer the consequences of doing so. Oh, how Eye want you to be strong enough to have self control over your bodies, hearts and minds and make decisions that will benefit you in the long run.

These are 5 steps that Eye want you to do and to consider when you feel that you are about to loose self-control.

1. **Draw a mental picture.** A simple illustration to help you grasp the basics of self-control is to ask yourself to imagine a stop sign that must be obeyed before you leap into a situation.

2. **Cool down.** Encourage yourself to walk away from a frustrating situation for a few minutes to cool off instead of having an outburst if you don't get your own way.

3. **Identify the trigger.** Encourage yourself to think about what's causing yourself to lose control and then analyze it. Explain to yourself that sometimes the situations that are upsetting at first don't end up being so awful after all.

4. **Consider consequences and options.** Remind yourself to think about long-term consequences. Urge yourself to pause and evaluate upsetting situations before responding and talk through problems rather than losing control, slamming doors, or yelling.

5. **Set clear guidelines.** Be clear about your expectations and the amount of self-control you expect from yourself. For example: Just knowing what hurtful things you can say or do but you have to catch yourself because you have matured.

Eye will give you some women examples of their encounters of having self-control of three different cultures of people.

*"Patience is a virtue! Unfortunately, some people lack that virtue. Personally, I have a limited amount of patience. Like most people, I don't like to be judged unfairly and I hate it when people depend on me to do things that they can do themselves, especially when I'm busy. Generally I'm a nice girl, but I'm not perfect. Sometimes I become easily annoyed and irritated. Now this may sound irrelevant to you, but generally speaking, I think many of you know what I'm talking about.*

*I may not have patience but I do have self-control. These attributes sound very similar, but they're not. Someone who is patient can tolerate things WITHOUT getting angry or upset. However, someone who has self-control can control their impulses – meaning they can be angry or upset but they're able to refrain from acting on it.*

*I think that if you have a limited amount of patience or none at all it's at least important to have self-control. If you don't, you may do things that you will regret, and/or make the situation worse. For instance, you may lose your patience with a professor because they graded you unfairly on an exam, or with a co-worker because they're always telling you what to do. If you lose your patience and can't control your impulses and you start yelling at them or get physical, you're not going to solve anything and it will definitely make the situation worse. On the other hand, if you use self-control and calmly speak to the person you're irritated with, you'll likely have a much better result.*

*The moral of the story is… "If you don't have patience, at least have self-control". You'll definitely need these skills in school, at work, and in life in general. Patience is a virtue, but to me, self-control is too.*

-Erica

*"I think troubled relationships- if not resolved, leads to disease of ones level of emotional intelligence. In this way, a vicious cycle of: lack of self-esteem & self-control, spirit "closes" toward future emotional commitments as a protective defense mechanism. If your self-esteem has been affected negatively you will not feel that your "speaking out" is worthy to be heard. In addition, stress blocks one's cognitive ability to engage in the level of critical, reflective thinking that is required to speak your mind, while assertively conveying your position. Without that, you will not be happy. Happiness fades depending on the circumstance but Joy is what we should all seek. The joy of the Lord, which is the strength we need so that we can recognize and" rise up" out of the troubled relationship; regain emotional intelligence to "speak our minds in love" and live life with self-control. Finally One must feel good about who they are and know where their strength comes from before they can experience Joy and happiness!"*
        *-Revia*

This last story is from a  woman who has being struggling with self-esteem and self- confident issues from her pass experiences. Eye will not expose her name or photo. Maybe this will help someone who has a similar story that they can relate to.

She writes: *"I am a survivor of both sexual and physical abuse. I had a total breakdown at age 38. This was preceded by physical abuse at the hands of my mother, sexual abuse at the hands of my older sisters many friends, an alcoholic father absent most of my life, and being bullied at school. Weed and alcohol was introduced to me when I was 15. This was the greatest thing in my life at the time. I realized that there were a lot of kids out there that had experience abuses similar to mine. I left home at age 17 never to return to the home where I grew up until a year ago when my daughter moved into the apartment where most of my abuse happened. This was very difficult for me.*

*I married at age 21 to a man I thought had rescued me from all the abuses in my life. It was greatest time in my life 2 children I was at the top of the world. It was then I realized I married an alcoholic. I separate for a short time from him. I realized I was the only person who would take care of me. I went back to school, became a nurse had 2 wonderful children, moved away, and the verbal abuse started. I felt broken. What did I have to do to be accepted. I finally broke all the was. Feeling worthless was a familiar thing for me comfortable shoes once again. I lost everything, my job, my children, my life. It took me 9 years to realize I was worthy. I was not a bad person. Over the past 4 years I got my life back, reconnected with my children , got my nursing license back. I have literally been to hell and back.*

*I do have days when it is still a struggle and days when I thrive. I do have a very hard time trying to assert myself. People seem to take me the wrong way most times. I was never able to speak my mind as a child and became a people pleaser as an adult . I struggle, how can I change this? I am a strong woman I feel because no one could have survived what I have in my opinion. What advice could you give me to continue my forward progress because I never want to go back to that place ever again."*

*Chapter 5*
# "SEX, DATING, & LOVE RELATIONSHIPS

*"Boys frustrate me. I hate all their indirect messages, I hate game playing. Do you like me or don't you? Just tell me so I can get over you.*

### -Kirsten Dunst

**Sex:**

Eye hope you don't feel uncomfortable talking about sex with me, maybe no one never really sat down and really discussed or broke it down to you yet. If not, Eye will tell you anyway, so open your mind.

Sex is suppose to be a very beautiful and sacred thing. You should always cherish that moment when you are experiencing sex. Now days it seems like its more casual and popular to just go around and have sex with any and everybody that you find attractive. That is a very dangerous thing to do, especially with all these sexual transmitted diseases going around and unplanned pregnancies. The most appropriate thing to do is to wait until your married to give yourself to a man. Make your honeymoon a once in a lifetime experience. If you have given yourself up to every boy or man that you date what will you have left to give to your husband?

You must innerstand why you really want to have sex. Is it just your hormones or is it something you want to do just to make the boys like you more? Eye know you are coming to the age where you are curious and you want to experience the feeling, but trust me, it is worth the wait.....especially with the right person. With all the sex that is shown on television and played in the music today, sex can be very tempting. You must control yourself. Never focus on what everyone else is doing because most people are dealing with their own insecurities and demons that they are fighting with. So, why do you want to have sex and why do you think you are ready to do that? Answer yourself those questions.

Sometimes after you have sex with a person, it seems like you start to feel different about them.....sometimes in a bad way, like, was it really worth it? Or you may regret for having sex with that person. And trust me, people talk and before you know it, everyone knows that you have gave it up.

Eye don't know if you heard about Sexual Transmitted Demons before. If not Eye will break it down to you. This is not to scare you but to give you the reality of things. Every boy/man carry their own demons inside of them....even you....and every time a woman opens up her legs and let a man inside of her, she is taking in all of his feelings, emotions, and demons.

The reason why it seems like some of the women act crazy is because they have let so many demonic men inside of their vagina (temple) and it is affecting their spirit, character, and morality. When you have sex with so many men your vagina becomes scarred and you are no longer considered a woman anymore but rather something else. In ancient scriptures they have a name for that and that type of woman is not marriage qualified because she has become a curse.... (research more on that)

Sex will not comfort or take away the pain or fulfill that emptiness you are feeling inside. You are only adding fuel to your own pain that's causing you to be emotionally unstable. You are accepting & carrying other Men spirits and baggage inside of you when you open your legs up to them while letting them enter in. It's called Soul ties. You become one with that person.

*"Your body is a temple, not a visiting center for men."*

Back to these sexual demons and soul ties. Do you know that every time you have sex with someone you are actually having sex with all the people they have had sex before you? Whatever energy that they have gotten from that other girl or woman, they have absorb it and passed it to you. It's just like catching an STD. Your probably saying to yourself that this too much to take in, but this is very good information to know and you will innerstand while a lot of females are out of control.

You may be asking yourself, "What about oral sex?" Well oral sex can be somewhat similar on the sexual transmitted disease side. If you decide to do oral sex to someone, you be sure that this person is clean and they are not one of those guys that do the nasty with everyone. That's why it is best to wait until your married to do all that freaky stuff because you don't want to catch diseases in your mouth. Also allowing boys/men to go down on you is the same thing. You don't know where else their mouth has been and you are taking in all these different liquids inside of you that may cause you to be irritated down there. After that you will kiss the same person. You see, that's a lot of germs and bacteria that's going in your mouth. We are too busy getting our groove on where we don't even take the time to think about all of this. Eye am not telling you to stay away from every guy and that every guy has diseases, but just be careful. Try to know more of their background and past sex encounters.

Never do anything you don't want to do. Be proud of your behavior and always put yourself first. If anyone who threatens to not be your friend or not wanting to be your boyfriend based on you not giving them sex, is, by definition, not your friend or boyfriend and doesn't deserve to be in your universe!

Feeling hormones is normal, but the behavior you engage in because of this can change the whole course of your life. There are many ways of expressing affection that don't include sex. You can make out a lot by lots of hugging and clean kissing. Sometimes it is better to do it with your clothes on rather than risking pregnancy or catching a STD. You know what Eye mean....hunching each other if you feel you cannot control yourselves. Eye am just being real with you because when you are a teen, it's going to happen.

If you are sexually active, please use some type of protection. Eye really don't agree with birth control pills or shots because sometimes it effects your body in a bad way, but if that prevents you from having unwanted babies, be my guess.

Now, since we talked about the bad that comes with sex, let's talk about the good and educate ourselves on sex. Having sex is like submitting yourselves to that person and wanting to feel their soul inside of you. It is very intimate and relaxing, especially if you are doing it with someone you actually love and care for you. It is even better if they feel the same about you.

Here are a few women of different ages that Eye know personally that will share their experiences of sex and what it means to them in a good way.

### Antonette Holder

*"Individuals have different motives for sex: relief from stress, to have a sexual desire met and/or procreation. Personally, I use "sex" to sanction that bond that my partner and I have made, and to reunite. After departing for many hours, sex brings us back to that oneness that I never want to lose. It is, also, satisfying to know that I have satisfied someone else. When I want to be pleasured, I call that sex. When I want pleasure with oneness, I call that making love. I literally use those terms for my husband to know what I want. I've had sex and then I've had love made to me. Just isn't the same. Real love making/sex is experienced within a loving relationship. I am talking about making love that touches every core of one's existence and brings one to tears. As the participants learn what the partner's likes and dislikes are, he or she will notice that as the days, months and years go by; making love/sex gets even better. When that is achieved, then the individuals involved will be able to go to different realms."*

### Kawaya

*"Okay I'm just going to say this as X RATED AND AS REAL AS POSSIBLE.... The feelings of sex is amazing, not just the penetration that pushes into your vagina, but before that the nipple sucking, titty licking, tongue kissing, booty caressing, etc, etc. Lots of good things about sex, but there are also a lot of bad things about sex. So pick the right person to give yourself to because u might think "it's just sex" but their*

*inner demons are coming through and emotions get attached and you might be left heartbroken and sad.. so never let someone who hasn't showed you who they really are into your pure amazing place where it should be respected and treated as a place of Worship..."*

**Yasmeen Brown**

*"I feel like sex is art. It's an expression of how deeply two can show just how much they are desired. But like most things you have to be mindful of the people you allow access or it can cause a negative effect. But yea, so in conclusion, sex is an enjoyable act. Just have to be aware of when not to engage in it."*

***Raven Royal***

*"Sex is a sacred act and should never be done loosely. Sex is spiritual and with the right person it can be great! It's not just a physically a good feeling (for women it tends to be more emotional) but emotionally it can feel a high that you don't wanna come down from, when it's RIGHT. Because women are more emotional we need to be careful in considering who we choose to share the most treasured parts of our bodies with. A girl should NEVER have sex to feel validated from a man or accepted from a man. We should NEVER under any circumstance have sex for the need for a man to like us. If you're gonna do it, do it because it's what YOU want to do not him. If a man says things like " if you liked me, cared about me, wanted to be with me then you would give it up (before you are ready) then he*

*probably doesn't like, care or really want to be with you beyond that moment. Men can be very manipulative and slick in the way they go about trying to convince you to give them the one thing that YOU have control over. You need to check your meter (mind) and ask yourself a few things before you decide to have sex with anyone.*

1. *Am I doing this because it's what I want to do?*
2. *Do I feel pressured in anyway to have sex?*
3. *Do I feel comfortable?*
4. *Do I have a connection (emotionally and spiritually) to this person?*
5. *Will I feel bad about myself and regret what I have done after we are finished?*
6. *Do I trust this person?*
7. *Am I mature enough to handle what comes with sex ? All these things considering that I know the person and have a friendship and/or relationship. If any of these answers are NO then you should NOT have sex because you are not ready and this isn't the right person to be having sex with. Treat your sexual organs like you treat the most sacred and important thing you have (because it is, besides your mind). No one should get that part of you if they don't deserve it."*

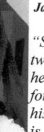

**Janet Okolo**

*"Sex is the song of the heart. It is a song of two soul merging the melody of each other heart. When a man heart is filled with love for a woman, she will feel every melody of his heart through every layer of her body. Sex is only beautiful thing and can be a cherishing memories, if a man you beyond the physical realm and crown you as his queen, by putting the ring on you."*

***Whitney Nicole***

*"Sex, to me, is beautiful because it serves so many Divine purposes. It creates a way for love to be expressed beyond the physical realm, a way for souls to combine, "exchange" or simply release - all in the midst of physically, emotionally & spiritually connecting.....something so special that through this experience only, life can be created. Talk about DIVINE! Sex is... perhaps a pleasant "escape" even, an experience so intimate that it can literally feel like you're "out of your own body". It can serve as food to the soul - healing & nourishing - after letting yourself go...melting into pure ecstacy."*

***Dominique Berridge***

*"Sex to me is more than a physical act... it is an act of trust on so many levels. For ME if I decide to be intimate with a person I am trusting you with my physical, my mental, and my emotional well being. Why is that? Because we connect and interchange energy on all those levels. What is in you is now in me and vice versa weather it be good or bad we are now one."*

**Dating & Love Relationships:**

Almost every relationship starts off great and you may have thought that you found your Prince Charming. In the beginning that boy or Man is trying to be everything that you approve of so he can have the privilege to get what he truly wants. After he succeeds, he tends to relax more and doesn't feel that he needs to try as hard. Then you will start to see his true characteristics.

You will find yourself feeling like you have been played or used. You have given this guy everything that you had to offer even though he is not your husband. So, in his mind, he keeps you tagging along until he finds something better while knowing that you cannot give him anything different or better than what you have been giving him.

What that being said....stop giving these guys all of you at once. If you are giving your all to every guy you think you are in love with, what will you have to give to your husband? Take your time!

That is why it is best to start going out on dates with different guys before jumping into serious relationships. Before you decide to go on any date, make sure that you are secure of yourself and that you are not hooking up with boys for the wrong reasons. This is a quote to live by and to to tell yourself before deciding to date:

*"I am more than just a woman. I am of and for God, and if you can't come to me as divine, then don't come to me at all."*
*-Mayahausca*

**Dating:**

As a young teenage girl you are getting curious now and you are wanting to experience a boyfriend. All of that is normal and Eye know you have been witnessing all of your friends getting boyfriends, but do not feel left out or think something is wrong with you just because you do not have one at the moment. Most teenage girls are just throwing themselves at these boys just to say they have a boyfriend. Please do not be one of those girls. Eye will give you some tips when it comes to dating and choosing the right kind of boys....this will even be helpful to older women too. Let me correct that..... honestly there isn't any right kind of teenage boys at the moment because at your age boys are going through puberty and their hormones are out of control. Half the rime their mind is only on one thing and that's making out or trying to break their virginity with someone.....so be careful on that. You may run into a few teenagers with their mind right but not many.

First off, never choose a boy who doesn't notice your inward beauty first. If a boy tell you that you are so beautiful and fine that he have to make you his girlfriend, then you cannot take him seriously. Eye am saying this because he is only showing you that he only wants you for your looks. The question is.....what happens when he runs into someone who he thinks looks better than you? A good choice of guy to be with is the one who will always give you good eye contact when talking to you and will look deeply into your heart and tell you that he loves your personality. He will let you know that he enjoys just being around you. You will know that he finds you beautiful but he will hardly tell you because he is not only focused on your outer beauty. He is actually trying to get to know you. Don't except anything less than a guy who appreciates your inner beauty.

Next, never let these guys objectify you. Meaning, never let them put you upon a pedestal just because of your looks and how your body is shaped. Especially if they think you are insecure or you don't think much of yourself. They will be so flattering with their words and make you feel like you are the most beautiful woman on the planet. Be careful, because there is a catch to that. If that is the only thing that they are focus on and talking about, they are only doing that to butter you up to get what they really want. Once that have you gullible and blushing, that's when it's easier for them to make their move. So Eye say that to sat this.....Know how beautiful you are where no one can make you weak and foolish with their compliments.

Another thing, never fall for a guy just because he is good-looking. You are going to see a lot of good-looking boys/men all through your life so just calm down. Even the most handsome boys can have the most ugly personalities and characteristics. By choosing a guy just because of his looks can lead to the most stressful heartaches. You will have to worry about him lying and cheating on you all the times. In his teenage and young adult years, a lot of guys like to play games. They want to be the biggest player and to see how many pretty girls they can have on their team. So don't become a statistic.

Also when dating or if you find yourself being interested in someone, never get too comfortable with them calling you names. Some guys get too comfortable where they are trying to test you to see what they can get away with just to impress their friends. Most guys love that kind of control over their girlfriends. If this guy keeps calling you negative names or names that really doesn't fit your character, then eventually you will start to believe that you are those names that he is calling you. The songs that you hear that are popular on the radio that degrades women with these names are wrong. That is only for entertainment and record sales. Please do not accept those titles just to fit in or to consider yourself cool.

When deciding to date, never tolerate or accept any kind of abuse. Eye am not just talking about physical abuse where he is putting his hands on you but also mental and emotional abuse. Abuse can creep up on you as in name calling & controlling behavior. Never let the guy influence you to be guilty over something you know you didn't do. When a guy tells you he's sorry and continue to do the same things over and over and over again, that is your que to leave. Never stay dating someone like that because those wounds will never heal and they will become an attachment to the misery that will take forever to fade away.

Let's be real here, when you are in your teenage years and your dating.....boys are going to cheat. No matter how beautiful you think you are and how much faithful you think your boyfriend is, he's going to talk to other girls. That's the reality. It's up to you to just play the game with him and have other guy friends in your corner. If he tells you he's faithful and is not talking to any other girls, he is a bold face liar. He may not be having sex with them but he is communicating with other girls other than you, so don't stress yourself on that too much. If he is smart and is a good, honest guy, he will be real with you and tell you that he talks to other girls but will not put another girl before you. Guys only do what you allow them to do while dating them. So it's up to you to set the standard. So set them high!

Here's the most important painful lesson of all. There is no such thing as a perfect boy. That doesn't even exist. All boys, even people have their own shortcomings and flaws about their character and actions towards women. You will know if you have found the right guy because he will uplift you and make you want to be a better person and he will not tear you down. That's how you will know he's a keeper.

**Relationships:**

Okay, now let's talk about getting into relationships. Note that Eye said "Relationships" which is more advanced than just randomly dating someone just because you like them. Getting into a relationship means that you actually want to be with this person and only them. You are actually trying to build something and to see where it goes. Many people have different kinds of relationships that they decide to get in but one thing Eye know for sure that they want to be with the person they are with regardless the situation or what kind of relationship it is. So Eye guess Eye will be giving you the tips on the basic love relationship and how to make it healthy and less stressful.

**Don't have doubts or bring any negative baggage into a relationship:**

The Ultimate Tragedy Is A Man Scared To Let His Guard Down & A Woman That Refuses To Waste Her Time. Both Are Loving People But Are Fearful Of The Cost Of Being Hurt At The Expense Of Loving The Wrong One Yet Again.

Before we get into having a healthy and productive love relationship, lets talk about having the right mindset before going into one. As you get older you become more self sufficient and cautious of who you are in a relationship with. Sometimes you are hesitant to trust a man. If your motive is to use a man for what he has or what he can give you then it's best for you to not get into a serious relationship and to play with a man's heart, especially if he's a good guy. Your Karma will come back 10 times worst on you, so be careful. Eye have a quote for women that does that to good men.

"You talk as if you had a heart. Women like you have no hearts. Heart is not in you. You are bought and sold."

Also you must leave your baggage at the door...meaning, don't have negative thoughts or doubts coming into a serious love relationship with a good guy. You will only cause drama and insecurity throughout the relationship by accusing him of things he's really not doing. Sometimes you get what you think about all the time. If you doubt the relationship will last, don't enter in one until you have gotten over your past.

When you sense a red flag, but you dismiss it as paranoia because despite your bad experiences with men you really do want to see the best in people. But it turns out your paranoia was really your intuition and he was full of shit... and you played yourself... ...Once again...

Don't get it twisted no-good men do cheat in relationships, but you can also lead a man to cheat on you. A man feels that if he knows that you believe he is cheating when he isn't,....in his mind, he might as well cheat anyway. It may sound strange but Eye am telling you the real from a man's point of view. So what that being said, you have gotten what you wished for. You carried those negative energies into your relationship.

Let Anger, depression, bitterness, anxiety, hate, & vengeance be no longer apart of you, for you are the foundation and everything starts with you concerning the rise of your love relationship.

When you are use to getting hurt and experiencing bad relationships, you will tend to not believe or accept the guy or relationship, when things are going to good. Here's an example from a message Eye received on social media.

> I have this one particular gentleman who would treat me and give me the world my daughter and I but I hit myself with the "he's too nice" .... blah blah blah

> Lol...girl you trippen...your just afraid to be hurt again...you are still carrying that baggage from your last relationships....give him a chance, take things slow and pay attention...

Once again, leave that baggage behind and forgive those who hurt you in the past. If not, you will never love the same again.

**Never jump into a relationship over stereotype or what you think is acceptable:**

This message was commented on a post Eye made on social media.

**Tatianna Byrd**
I am a California native with a I am a slim build and I find that most black men would not approach me or take my seriously when I approach them. Alot of my black guys friends say that I look intimidating or jokingly say you aint got an ass! So that's why white boys want to talk to you. Even moving to the south same thing. What advice would you give a girl that has these types of relationships problems among their own race. They same thing still goes on lighter the better or she got to have an phat ass and large breast to be considered beautiful. I understand that everyone does not believe in this but people like to follow the crowd. how can we change that within our society? I see a slow progression but yet its slow.

So what do you do when it seems as if you feel that it would be better if you date someone of another race or culture just because you think that your own race doesn't find you attractive?

First off, you cannot determine a few bad seeds in your own culture or race that will make you think that they all feel the way. Yes, sometimes words hurt and it may get to you but you must remain poise in these situations because everyone is not the same and sometimes people just like what they like. Other races or cultures of people may appreciate you much more sometimes because they admire how different you are and they are not use of seeing that kind of beauty. Don't get too caught up at being flattered by other cultures of people. You might just become an experiment for them of becoming a first, just to be tried out. Trends are created all the times within the people, especially what kinds of girls to get in relationships with. So please don't just accept someone else just because you feel that a certain kind of person do not want you. If you do, you will find yourself in a very submissive and abusive relationships and the guy that you are with will sense your insecurities, and he will take advantage of you.

Listen closely....some guys like small women, some like big women. Some even like women with big and small body parts, so don't stress yourself trying to fulfill every man's desire. A man can be so insecure within himself that he will do his best to make you feel just as low as him. Trust me, there are a lot of women who have their different preferences of the guys they date. Everyone does it at one a point of time in their lives, even you. No matter how the guy looks, his personality and character is most important. His look, race or culture means nothing if he's not treating you right or doesn't know how to be in a relationship. So don't rush into just being someone's trophy or trying to make them your trophy. Looks can be very deceiving.

Eye don't care how you look or what a few people have to say about you. Love your body and if you are not satisfied with it, put in the work to change it to your approval, but do it for yourself first before you decide to do it for a man or anyone else.

If you are one of those women who thrives off that stereotype that you are an independent woman and you do not need a man, then being in a relationship is not for you. You cannot come into a relationship having that kind of mindset because you will always try to find ways to leave when your love one makes you mad. You will always find yourself saying the same things to him like "Eye don't need you, Eye can take care of myself." Real relationships are not just about taking care of each other....it's about building with one another.

*Jasmine Chambers writes.... "A Strong, Independent Black Woman......"Not a compliment! I need a man. A strong hardworking respectful loving protector! I can't do this alone and I won't even try. This was drilled in the black woman head about 1954 when they took the focus off Black segregation and made it about women rights! NOPE! My eyes are open and you can no longer control me with society. I'm NOT a independent woman! I'm dependent on my BLACK MAN to lead me! That's the purpose. FYI! We are the only ones screaming women independence! White women marched and encouraged this with these black women then went home to their husband and kids and did exactly what she was supposed to! Can't you tell in the way our kids turn out ✊?✊build BLACK FAMILIES"*

**The difference between being in love and being attached in a relationship:**

Try not to confuse "attachment" with "love". Attachment is about fear and dependency, and has more to do with love of self than love of another. Love without attachment is the purest love because it isn't about what others can give you because your empty. It is about what you can give others because you are already full.

Ladies, do you really love these people that you are with? Are you just attached to them or is they attached to you?

If some people were where they wanted to be in life at the

moment, they would have different companions and wouldn't be with the person their with now. Only real and pure love keeps that bond strong, no matter what.

Eye have seen and heard a lot of stories of women being attached in relationships because of knowing the man they are with for several years and they feel that they can't find anyone better. It's like they surrendered or they are too drained to even leave the relationship to jump into another one. Another episode of being attached to some one is when an unplanned pregnancy or child is already involved in the picture. Many women feel that they should just hang on to their child's father and accept anything that he decides to do, just so he won't leave her and their children. That is not love, that is an attachment, especially if he doesn't really want to be with you. Never be afraid to be alone. There is a difference from being alone than being lonely.

This kind of attachment goes on a lot. The man know in his mind that he will never marry or fully commit to his woman so he gives her an engagement ring, better known as the "shut up ring". Don't get me wrong, not all men does this, but you will know when your man is full of it by the way he treats you in the relationship. He may love you but he is not so in love with you where he rather to give up the world just for you. He is just attached to you so much that he cannot stand for another man to try to sweep you of off your feet. So in his mind, by giving you this ring, most men probably will just bag away and figure that you are taken.

Engagement is when a man promises to marry a woman in a few months,not when he puts a ring on her finger and scares other men away for the next 5 years...that is witchcraft!!!

Don't be that woman who the man only tags along until he finds something better. Men get insecure as well and will be attached to you only because he feels that no other woman wants him, but as soon as he gets his confidence back up, you will start to see the change in him and that's when the other woman will start to pop up out of nowhere.

As you being a woman, Eye know that most of you would rather have that ring on your finger regardless of how independent and hard you pretend to act. Most women just come up with excuses to not want to marry because they know their own Men won't marry them. So they continue to cut pieces from their own heart. It's sad that some Men are taking that

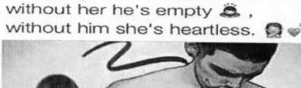
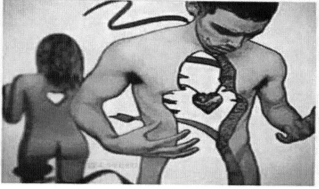

life away from our women. It's like they are taking your breath away while you gasp for air on a daily basis. So you settle to have babies to try to fulfill that desire of being complete or loved.

A lot of women will not be honest with their men to actually tell them that they really want this, because she has lost RESPECT for their men and they do not trust them anymore. Their love have become nothing more than an attachment to them. Eye know it makes them feel some type of way when they see their friends or others getting married, but hey, what do Eye know?

Be aware of men purposely impregnating you. A lot of guys do this to their girlfriends when they start to get the feeling that their girl might leave them. They believe that if they get you pregnant then chances are that you will not leave him. That is not love, just another form of attachment. Men even do the same thing to keep other men from coming around you. They will use terms like, "Eye don't want another man around my baby."

**Building the right love relationship:**

Love Relationships are not chosen or picked out specifically. Relationships are built on strong foundations. A lot of love

**Relationships Are Failing today because you are Building them on Weak Foundations.**

relationships fail because they were built on weak foundations and are only started because one was impressed by a particular cause of the moment. Today it seems like most people want everything fast and already put together and wrapped nicely. Most people have forgotten how too build relationships. This is why most women are so quick to call it quits the moment she sees something she doesn't like or if she sees things getting to hard to handle. It is so easier to quit on someone when things get bad, but you cannot continue this routine if you plan on being in any future relationships, especially if you desire to get married. Relationships are not perfect and at times they will get very hard but your love and commitment to one another will wither any storm if it is real and meant to be.

The time is now when you should be building the right foundations with those who stimulate you mentally, spiritually, and then physically. Having all those things will influence your relationship to last longer. You have to stop doing things backwards. Stop praising your boyfriends in the beginning of your relationships and giving your all to these people and having babies by those same people who are not committed or in Unity with you. This will only cause more broken homes and more abortions.

From a Man's point of view, when you start to praise your boyfriends in the relationship like he is your dream come true, it makes him ease back as in him not trying hard anymore. He knows that he finally got you where he wants you. He knows whatever he does, you ain't going nowhere.

When building your relationship you have decided that you and your Man is not perfect and that he is worth building something with. You cannot expect perfection all the time. What you need to really focus on is effort from him. Even if he fail at times (and he will), you must not down him or kick him when he needs your support. Even you, must put in the same effort as him. Remember, the effort that you put into your relationship is the effort you will receive from it.

Here are some tips on building a strong, balanced, love relationship......

Create a safe environment with one another where you can trust and share openly without any fear or being uncomfortable. Don't interrupt, even if you need to put your hand over your mouth to stop yourself. Learn to fight fairly. No name calling. Don't make threats. Also you have to learn to push your pride and ego to the side to apologize when you know you should. If you're too angry to really listen, stop! Go into another room, take space for yourself, breathe, and calm down. Remember, your partner is not your enemy.

Separate the facts from the feelings. As a woman you will tend to be in your feelings more because women tend to be more emotional. Ask yourself: Is there something from my past that is influencing how I'm seeing the situation now? The critical question you want to ask: Is this about him or me, or is it really about me? What's the real truth? Once you're able to differentiate facts from feelings, you'll see your partner more clearly and be able to resolve conflicts from clarity.

Connect with the different parts of yourself. Each of us is not a solo instrument. We're more like a choir or an orchestra with several voices. What is your mind saying? What is your heart saying? What is your body saying? What is your "gut" saying? For example: My mind is saying "definitely leave him," but my heart says "Eye really love him." Let these different voices or parts of you co-exist and speak to one another. In this way, you will find an answer that comes from your whole self.

Also you have to develop compassion. Practice observing yourself and your partner without judging. Part of you might judge, but you don't have to identify with it. Judging closes a door. The opposite of judging is compassion. When you are compassionate, you are open, connected, and more available to respectfully communicate or debate with your partner. As you increasingly learn to see your partner compassionately, you will have more power to choose your response rather than just reacting.

Create a "we" rather than making it about you. The foundation for a thriving, growing, mutually supportive, love relationship is being separate, yet connected. In unity relationships, each person sacrifices part of him or herself — compromising the relationship as a whole.

You have to be able to heal yourself when wounded individually. Don't expect your Man to always fill your emotional holes, and don't try to fill his. Ultimately, each of us can only heal ourselves. Your Man, however, can support the journey as you work with yourself, and vice versa. In fact, living in a loving relationship is healing in and of itself.

The differences between you and your partner are not negatives. You don't need a relationship with someone who shares all of your interests and views. We may sometimes fear that these differences are incompatibilities, but in fact, they're often what keeps a relationship exciting and full of good fire.

All too often, we make up our own stories or assume about what our Man's behavior means. For example: "He doesn't want to cuddle; he must not really love me anymore." Just be open and ask questions.

Make time for your relationship. No matter who you are or what your work is, you need to nurture your relationship. Make sure you schedule time for the well-being of your relationship. That includes making "play dates" and also taking downtime together. Frequently create a sacred space together by shutting off all things. Like a garden, the more you tend to your relationship, the more it will grow.

Last but not least, say the "hard things" from love. You know the saying, "Eye rather hurt you with the truth, than make you comfortable with a lie." Become aware of the hard things that you're not talking about. How does that feel? No matter what you're feeling in a situation, channel the energy of your emotions so that you say what you need to say in a constructive manner.

When building and holding on to your relationship, you must keep this in mind: If you are in a serious relationship or married....Eye know sometimes you may feel like your missing out on what's going on in the world while you sit back and see all these other single women having fun going out and partying. It's normal to feel that way sometimes, so don't trip out or stress on that. Just remember....the grass on the other side it's not always greener. What you might be seeing is just an illusion because most of these single women would love to have what you have and be willing to trade places with you any day. They are still searching for that one person to slow them down so they can finally exhale because believe it or not, they are tired. So don't be deceived. What you have is value and the things out in the world doesn't contain any value at all. So don't be stupid and give up a kingdom for a cheap thrill.

What that being said, you have to keep building. Also you don't want to rush something that you want to last 4ever. Take your time, and finding real Love has no time or age limit to it, so never feel that it is too late or too early for you. Just let things flow and never give a person all of you until they are ready to make it all the way official as life partners and soul mates. You just worry about staying beautiful inside and out. Keep loving yourself so you can be so secure to love someone and to be loved in return.

*"Your Love Relationship is determined on how much you really love yourself. If you are insecure and have doubts about yourself, you will tend let your Man take advantage of you and abuse you mentally, emotionally, and physically. You will continue to forgive him and let him back into your life, over and over, and over again, until you learn to really love yourself to say, "ENOUGH IS ENOUGH!!!"*

*Chapter 6*
# "FRIENDS"

***"Lots of people want to ride with you in the limo.....what you want is someone who will take the bus with you when the limo breaks down."***
***-Oprah Winfrey***

**Grade-school Friendships:**

While you are in middle school and especially in highschool, is when you will start to actually care about having friends. This is the time where you are trying to fit in where you fit in. During this time you are still trying to find yourself. You tend to compare yourself to your friends and to try to be notice by the poplar girls or the cool boys. In this case, you will have to learn to just be yourself because trying to keep up just to remain friends with someone is hard work. Never let anyone of your friends influence you to do anything to get you in trouble, regardless if they tell you that they are not going to be your friend anymore if you refuse. If that's the case, then they're not really your friend anyway. You have to look out for yourself at times because you are left alone while dealing with the consequences.

A good friend to have is those kind of girls who are quiet and stays to themselves from time to time. You know, the ones who don't really follow the crowd. During school times, you can really get yourself into some trouble that will still have effect on you growing up, so be careful who you choose to be your friend.

Have you ever had a friend where you have to pretend to like the things they like and become an ugly person just to hang with them? If so, you need to end that friendship now. Find that friend where you can just talk about anything with and not be judged. A good friend is all about trust and loyalty. You don't want to second-guess whether you can tell your friend something. True friends are like diamonds....their bright, valuable, and always in style.

Just because your friend has a boyfriend doesn't mean that you have to have one. Just because your friend curses doesn't mean that you have to curse too. A true friend will accept you for who you are and will not make fun of you when you don't do what they decide to do. They will respect you for being different if they actually cared. They will never put you into a situation knowing that you are uncomfortable with it. In highschool some girls have no heart and will set you up for failure. They can get very competitive and jealous at times especially if you are getting the attention that they want. You can try on a certain outfit and be skeptical about it but that jealous friend will tell you that it is beautiful, just so people can talk badly about you.

Beware of that friend who loves drama and loves to gossip. If she spends time talking bad about people while smiling in these same people faces, then she is doing the same exact thing to you behind your back.

**Lisa Lyric Justice**
I've always been a social outcast.I was severely picked on in high school by people who I thought were friends,to the point where I decided to drop out of school.I Don't have many friends I have one..and we fall out from time to time but we have always been open and honest with each other.I'm use to people talking shit about me because I'm different.

When these toxic friends start to effect your day to day life and your school work, then it becomes a big problem and you must walk away from them.

The screen shot comments are real live conversations Eye had with women that Eye know personally on social media, excuse the typos.....

**Dominique Bey**
The same with me Lisa lyric on the social outcast part! I never had too many friends or cared to make many which explains why I only had that one best friend threw grade school/highschool! I can't stand messy females, envying females or drama rats! Eye don't like force friendships either! Eye have elevated so much into the point where eye disappeared on certain people without explaining anything! Friendships/sisterhood to me is about building each other up, telling the truth about one another even if it hurts! Seeking improvement! Just being there for one another and it never being one-sided!

When Eye was in school Eye witness so many girls destroy and bring down their friends. It's like they had some kind of attachment and control on them. These relationships are stronger than any kind of relationship with your boyfriend because your friend will want to know all of your business and if he doesn't meet to her approval, she will do any and everything to destroy your relationship. She will tend to get jealous at times and feel that you are spending more time with your boyfriend rather than with her. Highschool girls tend to get jealous a lot....Eye don't know why, but they do. Maybe it's because of insecurities within themselves. A real friend will always be happy for you and your relationship and will not try to be all up in your business while telling you what you need to do. She will always be a listening ear whenever you decide to vent to her about your problems.

In school there will be a lot of parties to attend and believe me when Eye tell you that your friends will try to drag you to all of them and will probably talk bad about you if you decide not to go with them. It's okay to hang out every now and then but do not make it a habit where you are breaking dates with other people just to satisfy them.

Remember some people mature quicker than other sometimes and what is fun for them may not be fun to you anymore.

**Friendships, while elevating in your womanhood:**
**(The Good, The Bad & The Ugly)**

**Jandry C.**
My definition of a real friend is an
unconditional friend. I can't stand drama,
which is usually sisters being too emotional
or immature. If something bothers you, just
tell me straight up. Don't tell someone else
or hold grudges if your supposed to be my
real friend. I have a couple of real close girl
friends but none that live around me or that I
see regularly. I feel that as I grow I have that
desire to find some real women that are on
the same page as me to really have that
support that we need as sisters. But it's so
hard to find.

**Kamelia Bey**
My best friend keeps it one hundred with me
no matter if it hurts me or not. But always
uplifting and sharing new ways to make me
better spiritually first n mentally physically n
socially as well. My best friend just cane in
my life n I recognized her by her fruits. I
don't have a lot of friends but when I do they
are always valuable to me. I don't like lazy,
drama, gossip, haters, so I don't be atound
most women

**Theresa Jones**
To me it's a person Like my sister herself
who's been where I've been, someone you
can call when thing's get ruff when thing's
aren't going right, it's more than just a family
member, But a forever friend that keeps a
Bond 💯 % one who don't Flip Flop. One who
ain't Fake. One who always have my back
and I Dan sure got yours. That's me and my
sister. 👯 👯 👯 👯 ✊✊✊✊✊

Some women are bitchy, toxic and competitive. And that's okay too. You don't have to like every single woman you meet. Just remember not to get carried away with hating them.

Don't tear other women down even when your friend tries to tear you down, because even if they're not your friends, they are women and this is just as important. This is not to say you cannot criticize other women, but understand the difference between criticizing constructively and tearing down cruelly.

Some women will probably be the first to put their hand up and say that they applied some shocking cruelty to other women in the past - mostly when they was younger, but it's still not an excuse. You may have done and said things that you deeply regret, even when you still continue to dislike the person in question. No one's perfect and everyone gets caught up in emotions from time to time. But always remember this...."She is not the enemy. She is never your enemy."

Let's face it, women already have to put up with enough name calling, undermining, professional harassment, slut shaming, victim blaming and general bull**** from the World At Large. You guys don't need it from each other.

If you are the kind of woman who says, "I'm mostly friends with guys," and act like you're proud of that, like that makes you closer to being a man or something and less of a woman as if being a woman is a bad thing, fix it. It's okay if most of your friends are guys, but if you praise this as a commentary on the nature of female friendships, well, soul-search a little.

Once again women at times are annoying, bitchy, competitive, and toxic. Men are just simpler, and that's why some women prefer to be friends with males rather than females. Some of you may have female friends that probably outnumber the guys about 6 to 1. Maybe even more. Embrace your friendships with women. Gain the solidarity, the connection, the support. Sometimes Eye see how hilarious most of them are. Women are BOSS. If you're not friends with any women, just try it out for a bit and see how you feel. Oh and Eye am not talking about the females who are evil and always walking around with tricks up their sleeves.

If you and your friends are in the same field or on the same level.....you can collaborate or help each other, do this without shame. It's not your fault that some of your friends are awesome. They may even be more awesome than you....don't hate that or get jealous.

Don't flirt, have sex, or engage in emotional affairs with your friends' boyfriends or ex-boyfriends. This shouldn't need to be said, but it needs to be said. Your friends' ex is most of the time an asshole, and you don't want to be involved with an asshole who's used goods. If you want to be with an asshole, get a fresh asshole of your very own. They are many out there. This causes a downfall and trust issues within female friendships.

Some women recognizes and value their worth from the positive, sexual praise of others but it comes at the expense of other women. Don't be that woman. You know, the one who flirts with her friend's main squeeze because it makes you feel good to think that if you really wanted it, you could have him. You are being an enemy to other women.

**Tolu Omar**

*"My fellow black women we need to learn to GET ALONG!! Yes everyone should get along but I'm talking about us now. Not everything is a competition, an issue, or whatever! Stop giving your fellow sisters dirty looks, fighting, talking mess and etc,etc. There will come a time when we will have no choice other than to come together! Life is so much bigger than the bullshit!*♥ *"*

Within your friendship with your girlfriends, have you ever felt like they were so attached to you where you couldn't even go anywhere alone without them saying "Why you didn't tell me that you were going there?" This happens a lot between girls where they feel that they are obligated to know your every move and if you do not let them know, they will feel that you have betrayed them.

Eye have heard several stories and witness these situations involving friendships between women on how attached they are with one another. Some women do not even go to college because of their friends.....Some do not even get married because of their friends. Eye can go on and on. You should never allow your friends or even your best friend to hold you back in life from achieving your goals or dreams.

You will have those type of friends that will support you on doing negative things that will destroy you like drinking, smoking, sex with different guys, etc,etc....but will not support you on any positive things that will cause you to grow into a better person. Why is that? Eye do not know but it happens a lot. Like Eye have said before, women get jealous of other women and they will do anything to keep you on the same level as them. As soon as they see that you are elevating past them, you will see the change in their behavior towards you. Remember, misery loves company, so never entertain miserable people.

If they are your real friends they will be proud of you and admire your maturity and elevation and it will be up to them to bridge that gap. Never elevate yourself downwards to satisfy your friends but rather let them elevate themselves upward to walk with you in maturity and in success. If you decided to keep stooping down just to satisfy someone or to keep a friendship, then you will eventually stay down there and mess up the things that you have in your life that are going good for you. So be very careful on that.

Do your friends stand up for you in front of other people. Do your friends hang around people that she knows that doesn't like you you? Do your friends entertain the negative conversations about you?

Those are questions that you need to ask your friends and you need to know the actual truth about this. This can lead to a lot of drama in your life if you have messy friends who plays around with people who she knows that doesn't like you for whatever reasons. Then some may have the audacity to invite you to places with those same individuals just to see the response they get from you. You have to keep it real with your friends and be very outspoken and straight forward on things like this. Let them know what you will not tolerate.

 **JoAnne Boyd**
Its not a race thing its a female thing I hear so many women go through the same thing, she's a hater, she's this, she's that, but I experienced females who would talk ish about one female but would be in her face the next minute, or simply would hate on someone for something they have or a man so I just don't socialize with certain females with bitter and hateful attitudes bc I just can't deal with the immaturity.

*"Folks will blow up your phone when they need something from you, but will not even call just check on you just to see how you are doing."*

These are the 5 types of girl (friends) to avoid:

## 1."The Crazy Bitch"

We all know a crazy bitch, (Eye am not trying to disrespect any female and Eye do not use this word at all, but these women actually refer to themselves as that.)-- she's the one who's loud and is quick to fight someone. She is that friend who is always back in forth in and out of your life because she got pissed at you over something petty. She is also the one who will bust out the windows of your boyfriend's car if she knows he's cheating on you. She starts drama wherever she goes, its like she pisses people off as soon as she looks at them.

It's natural that you want to save this friendship, because she's very fun, outgoing, and spontaneous. She probably was normal and happy once-- she didn't need to be sedated or tied up in a strait jacket. Her descent into insanity was gradual, hardly noticeable, until one day, she throws a bottle at your face, and suddenly, it hits you: She's flown over the cuckoo's nest! So, you may want to be careful when hanging around this kind of friend. You don't have to completely cut her off, at least get her some help.

## 2."The Negative Nancy"

She's the one that catches a cold and swears she has caught an STD from someone for sure she has an STD. She is most likely to tell you that you are pregnant every time you have unprotected sex. She will always think about the bad consequences in every situation.

For her, everything is the worst-case scenario, which means getting a hang nail means she'll have to amputate her finger or someone cutting her off on the freeway means she's the worst driver on the planet. You find that your friendship has devolved into soothing her fears and concerns and rubbing her back as you wait for another mental breakdown to occur, just two exits away. She tends to be paranoid about everything.

While it's important to take care of your friends, the "Negative Nancy just robs you of your emotional support, and what do you get in return? Conspiracy theories and a lot of trips to the pharmacy. It's time you write your own prescription and end this toxic relationship.

### 3. *"The Rich Spoiled Brat"*

It's difficult not to despise the girl who has everything, because in addition to being gorgeous, rich, thin, fashionable and smart, she's also probably really nice (or great at pretending to be.) She might even be a princess, which really makes us want to kill her. Once in a while, jealousy still rears her ugly little head and your lack of job, American Express Black Card and 7-series BMW becomes more and more apparent. Not only does her having everything affect your self-worth, but it may also cause you to become critical (talk crap) of your friendship. If you can keep your emotions in check, then great for you, but if you're in a particularly less advantageous state of affairs, having this kind of friend may reiterate just how unfair life actually is.

She is the one who looks down on everyone because of their lack of finances or lack of material things. She never wears the same thing twice within a monthly period and will always be your biggest critic on how you dress. You will go broke dealing with this kind of friend, while spending money on expensive things that you really don't even need. You will think that she doesn't even know how it feels to be without.

### 4. *"The Party Girl"*

Channeling Lindsay Lohan, Paris Hilton, Love & Hip-Hop girls, and the rest of the female Hollywood brat pack that's known for drunk driving, pouting for mugshots and having very little talent. These ladies are all versions of the party girl-- she's fun, pretty, gets into all the coolest parties, and for some miraculous reason, is still friends with you. But wait. She's calling you from the police station at 3 a.m. to come bail her out of jail, and it's your new dress that she spilled her fourth Red Bull vodka all over (without an apology). That's because the party girl doesn't care very much about anything but the party, and for her, maintaining a friendship simply means she has someone to enter or exit a party with. In reality, your just one of her sober and designated drivers. Bounce this fake friendship from the club and keep your finances and fashion intact. This friend will eventually turn you into an alcoholic or worst.

## 5. *"The Copy Cat"*

Be careful of this friend....she is the type that will try to steal your style, fashions and creativity and take the credit for it. She watches your every move and deeps down inside she really envy you.

She is also kind of weird and you may think that she is a lesbian or is just obsessed with you or something. She looks like an individual, but she is just a carbon copy of your opinions and preferences. Ask her what she wants to do, and she'll respond enthusiastically with her favorite phrase: "Whatever you want!" For a minute, you would think that she is your boyfriend the way she is attached to you. If she sees you getting attention from boys or a certain group of cool people, she will dress up exactly like you while imitating your character towards others. It's kind of creepy. This is the kind of friendship that you want to cut short before they get in to deep with you.

### Signs of a Real Friend

• They never forget your birthday and always make sure that they get to see you, no matter what plans have already been made.

• If your car is off the road they will offer to drive you even if it means that they are going out of their way to do so, neither will they accept any petrol money from you for doing it.

• You can laugh together until you both have tears running down your face.

• You can sit in silence together and still feel comfortable.

• Even if you only see each other two or three times a year, when you are together it's like you have never been apart.

• They will tell you the truth even if it hurts because they love you.

• They won't just tell you the things that they know you want to hear to keep you happy.

• They will offer their unfailing support no matter what you try to do, even if they don't agree with your choices they will support you in them.

• When they offer you a compliment it is genuine and from the heart.

• They won't say anything behind your back or gossip about you when you are not there.

• They know what makes you happy, your favorite film, sweet treat, your dress size and what colors you prefer to wear.

• They will listen to you moan and rant and offer you a shoulder to cry on whenever you need it.

• They know about all of your insecurities but won't broadcast them to the masses.

• When you need advice they will offer straight talking sense.

• You find it hard to imagine your life without them in it.

Trust me, these friends do not come around too often, so cherish them.

## Signs of a Fake Friend

• You have never felt comfortable enough with them to tell them a secret.

• They have never asked about your family and you have never shared any details of your family with them.

• You normally only spend time with them in a group setting, never on a one to one basis.

• They have never seen the real you, they only see the fake image that you put on when you are part of the group.

• They forget your birthday and other important dates.

• You often get the impression that they are only calling you because no one else was available.

• You laugh and have fun but it's not that feel good, belly aching laughter.

• You have never seen each other cry.

• You find it difficult to be yourself when you are around them.

• Any silences between you are awkward and you feel the need to fill them with conversation.

• If you don't see each other for a few months you would probably forget they existed at all.

• It can feel as though your relationship is all one sided – you are making all the effort.

• They talk about your insecurities in public and embarrass you.

• You find yourself agreeing with them so as to keep the peace and not get into an argument.

• It's easy to imagine your life without them in it.

**Raven Royal**
Through the actions of other sisters is what determines whether I hang around another female. I pay attention to how they treat the people that they say they love and respect. I pay attention to if they gossip and talk about people they claim they care about. I don't know what a fake friend is. In my eyes a friend cannot be fake otherwise I wouldn't use the word "friend" to describe them. A friend is someone that no matter how far or how many days, weeks, months go by and you may not speak with each other, you never have to question their loyalty and love because in your heart and mind you already know without any hesitation they will be there for you when you need them. A friend will always tell you the truth even if it may hurt their feelings. A friend is someone that will promote the best parts of you and enjoy watching you grow and become great. A friend sees the best and worst of you and love you regardless. I friend can tell you if they were not happy with something you did without getting defensive or angry. A friend will encourage you, or sit in silence with you. I friend keeps their word and promises.

*Chapter 7*
# OVERCOMING THE ABUSE, LONLINESS, PAIN, BETRAYAL & BITTERNESS

*"We may encounter many defeats but we must not be defeated."*
*"I can be changed by what happened to me. But I refuse to be reduced by it."*
*"There is no greater agony than bearing an untold story inside you."*
*-Maya Angelou*

-LET GO OF YOUR PAST-
**(The Meditation phase)**

Your past May be dragging you down and getting in the way of you manifesting your dreams. Sometimes you to learn a try a meditation within yourself to let go of old emotional and mental baggage that's keeping you unbalanced in life. Some of you may be hanging on to the pain of a lover who left you or you may experience a humiliation in loosing something or even you may have suffered scars growing up in your childhood that you haven't got over yet. These things hurt but they happened in the past. By you keeping the past alive, it makes it difficult for you to be open to new relationships and new opportunities in the present. To start this meditation it is better to be lying down and to cover yourself with a light blanket. Breathe deeply and relax for a minute. Even if you have to cry or shed a few tears thinking about the pain, do it, let it out. Bring to mind any emotional baggage and put it in your mind that it is time to let go. Visualize your emotions as an old, beat up suitcase you drag around wherever you go. Imagine letting go of the suitcase and your old pain..Convince yourself that these hurtful feelings, no longer serve you. Feel how much lighter you feel without it. Continue scanning your memory for old baggage, and old worn out hurtful emotions. Thank them for all the service they have given, but let them know it's time for you to let them go.

Visualize and feel yourself as lighter and free. Breathe deeply and relax for a few minutes. See your future opening before you, full of promise and opportunity. You must want and have a desire to let go of this pain and the chains that's holding you down because you will never rise up. You must talk about it. or it will continue to stay silent while eating you up inside.

(How to heal from Sexual Abuse) -A Start-

"The Yoni is a sanskrit Word meaning Womb or source....This Yoni meditation will help you heal from sexual violation and abuse you have suffered.

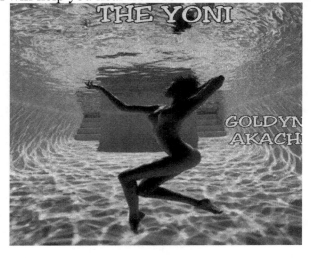

It will allow you to have a positive relationship with your body and your sexuality. Eye know it may seem hard ladies but we have to try. If you have suffered from sexual abuse, you probably have issues with shame. You might have developed negative feelings about your body and your sexuality. Meditating can help you recover. So please, try this.

First, lie down on a yoga mat or a made up pallet on the floor. Imagine you are taking a journey to a beautiful Goddess temple in another place and another time. Let your mind be free.

Imagine a Priestess(A higher Goddess) greets you as you arrive at the temple. She tells you how the door (womb) was damaged in the last invasion. Although the door(womb) has been replaced, there is a spiritual damage that needs to be healed. She calls on you to help her, because all women are made in the image of the Goddess and have their own secret doorways.

Imagine her asking you to put your hands on your body and think about how carefully, how gently, you would want your doorway(womb) to be opened. She goes to the door of the temple and prays to the Goddess with the words..."Eye love you, please let me in..."

Suddenly, the temple door opens a little and you can see the light shining and smell the incense from within. You enter and behold a Goddess. You approach the Goddess and tell her your deepest shame. She receives your shame with love and burns it in a ritual fire. As you leave the sanctuary, you know that you have received a healing deep within yourself that will unfold and manifest itself when the time is right...

Eye hope this will lighten the burden that some of you bear...but we must overcome it in order to continue to live and love again.....it all starts within you!

## Dealing with being Neglected by loved ones:

Whatever pain, heartache, hatred, or bitterness that you have, needs to be removed from yourself. If not, you will pass those same trials and tribulations to your seeds and they will become emotionally unstable with behavior issues. Especially to the women during their pregnancy. Your baby will feel everything that you are feeling and it will have an negative effect on them as well while growing up. Some of us have been affected as well from our parents, that's why we talk and act the way we do...some worst than others are very argumentative, negative, and drama brats. *Pain is relative*

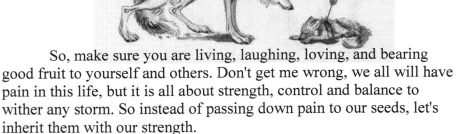

So, make sure you are living, laughing, loving, and bearing good fruit to yourself and others. Don't get me wrong, we all will have pain in this life, but it is all about strength, control and balance to wither any storm. So instead of passing down pain to our seeds, let's inherit them with our strength.

A lady that Eye know has been dealing with some REALLY, REALLY, HARD things Emotionally And Mentally. She cries herself to sleep often. She says that she have been in pain for sometime now and doesn't know how to disguise it. It is eating her up on the inside.

She doesn't get any Respect or Love from her older children, her son's father/spouse, one of her close friends, or even her own mother. She says that it hurts her so deeply that the people that she loves doesn't love her back, while she continues to love hard and deep. She goes above and beyond for those that she love but never gets it back in return. She tells me, "I am torn up, really I am. I go from day to day emotionally distraught, pretending to be okay."

She has a 4 year old who she loves within every bone in her body. Her son tells her all the time, "Mommy I Love You".....and she still feel a void from within.

She feels as if no one loves her and it hurts her so badly. She has tried so hard with her mom, her kids, her son's father, and her friend. It's like they don't want her love and don't want to love her the way she needs to be loved.

My response to her and to those that are dealing with something like this, just remember.......Damage people do not know how to truly love others in return. They are sent to destroy and tear other people down. Their misery needs company and you must never entertain it or feed your energy to them. Stay the person you are and never let them change you for the worst. It will get real hard and you may even feel lonely at times but your never alone. Just hang in there because there is a season for everything. Love, peace, and joy is approaching and if you allow yourself to be torn up inside, how would you recognize the award when it comes?

Being neglected or having that thought is the worst feeling in the world. It can become very depressing at times.

*These are some things to do that will help you overcome that neglected feeling:*

#1 First, take a look at yourself and your own behavior. Before jumping to any conclusions, take a minute to examine your own behavior. If your love ones are ignoring you, it might be due to something you inadvertently did to make them feel overwhelmed or uncomfortable. Maybe you are too clingy or too intrusive. It might just be that your partner needs a little space every once in a while.

#2 Look at the situation from their perspective. It could very well be that your loved one's lack of attention has nothing to do with you at all. Try seeing things from their point of view. Maybe they are simply busy, or don't feel well. Maybe they are tired or experiencing a distracting family issue. It's important to consider all possibilities when you're feeling neglected.

#3 Slow it down a bit. When you're feeling neglected, just give the other person a short break. Try not texting or calling them for an entire day. Or if you stay in the same house with them, just isolate yourself by only speaking whenever you are spoken to. This gives them a chance to miss you and text or call you first. By making yourself a little less available to your loved ones, you create an air of mystery about you that might lead them to wonder what you're up to.

#4 Get out of your own head. When someone ignores you, it's easy to become sad or even depressed. The best thing to do in a situation like this is to get out of your own head. Smile, be happy, and don't allow the other person's hurtful behavior to ruin your day. The happier you are, the more likely people are to be drawn to you. Confidence is sexy, so be the strong, confident type, and people will find you extremely hard to ignore.

#5 Remain independent. Always have a backup plan for those times when your loved ones aren't available. Go out with your friends or immerse yourself in a project. Throwing a pity party for one is no way to spend your valuable time and besides, it's good and healthy to keep a life that's independent of each other. It keeps you grounded, and having something to keep you busy stops you from over-thinking the situation.

#6 Be honest about how you're feeling. One of the best ways to figure out the situation and get past it is to confront the other person and simply be honest about how you're feeling. Come right out and ask them why they are ignoring you. Did you do or say something wrong, or is there some other reason? It could simply be that they have no clue they are neglecting you and that you are feeling this way. In this situation, honesty and kindness are key.

#7 Reconnect. Once you find out the reason for the neglect, you can begin to fix the problem. Try reconnecting with each other by talking about your passions and interests. Give each other ample time to talk and express yourselves without interrupting the other when they're on a roll. Ask questions and truly be interested in what the other person has to say.

#8 R-E-S-P-E-C-T. Demand it. If all of your attempts at being honest and reconnecting with each other fail to rectify your loved one's neglectful ways, let them know you will not be disrespected that way. Don't let them continue to get away with it.

*These are the things NOT to do when you're feeling neglected when you are dealing with all kinds of relationships:*

Don't:
#1 Accuse. Unless you're one hundred percent sure your partner is cheating on you, lying to you, or breaking the rules of your relationship in some way, never make accusations. Accuse your family of hating you when you have no proof. Doing so may push them even further away.

#2 Jump to conclusions. You might be totally convinced you know why your loved ones are ignoring you, but never assume. You know what they say about assuming, don't you? It makes an A-S-S out of yourself.
Do not jump to conclusions; you could be totally wrong, or not know the entire story.

#3 Ignore facts. If what your partner tells you it doesn't add up, pay attention. On the other hand, if your loved one conveys in some way that they want help, be conscious of that as well. Get the facts and be able to read between the lines, if necessary.

#4 Get defensive. Feeling neglected can certainly cause you to be angry and hurt, but don't get defensive. Whining, being needy, or trying to justify your behavior won't bring your loved ones closer to you.

#5 Play the victim. As much as your loved *one's* neglect feels like rejection, don't play the victim. Don't make the situation all about you, unless you know for sure it IS all about you.

## The PAIN of being Molested:
## (Speak Out)

### "Her Story"

It all started when Eye was 7 years old. My mother use to work overnight sometimes and my Father and Eye spent some nights alone. He help me with my homework from time to time when Eye needed help. When Eye was scared to sleep alone from watching scary movies, he was always there to tuck me in and keep me safe from the monsters under my bed.

My Daddy was really affectionate with me. He always use to

hug and kiss me often and Eye loved the attention. Eye felt that he loved me more than Mommy because all they did was yell and argue with one another. When mommy told me no, daddy was always there to the rescue to tell me yes, every time. Daddy use to watch a lot of movies with me where Eye saw men kissing girls and touching them. Daddy said that is what people do to each other when they love one another.

One night when Eye was all tucked in to go to sleep, daddy came into my room and laid in my bed. He got under the covers with me and told me he wanted to just lay here until Eye fell asleep. Daddy was so caring and he loved me so much. He rubbed my back and turned me around so I could lay on his chess. He then asked me do Eye love him and of course Eye said, "Yes, Eye love you very much." He then asked me do Eye remember what people do when they love each other. Eye told him Eye do. Then he kissed me on my lips while his hands were eventually all over my body. He told me that Eye was the most beautiful girl in the world. It felt weird kissing my daddy like that and Eye didn't know how to respond....Eye didn't know where to like it or to dislike it, so I just let daddy love me the way he showed me.

The next day, daddy went to work in the morning while mommy was just getting home. Later that afternoon mommy got up and we were in the living room playing and watching t.v. We then saw on t.v. where a man was kissing a woman and my mommy told me to close my eyes. Eye said, "Why mommy, daddy let me watch this all the time and he said that was people do when they love one another." She told me that is what grownups do, not kids. So Eye told her that was what me and daddy did last night in my room. Mommy got real mad and slapped me in my face and told me to never make up a lie like that again. But Eye told her Eye wasn't lying, just ask daddy. Mommy then, got real mad and told me to go to my room and wait until my father comes home.

Daddy is home and mommy is waiting for him in the living

room. Eye sneaked out into the hallway so Eye could here them talking. Mommy told daddy what Eye had told her and daddy started laughing. Mommy asked him did he do it. Daddy got real mad and start yelling at mommy and couldn't believe that she would ask him something like that. Daddy started yelling at mommy and was threatened her that he would leave, so mommy started crying and told him that she was sorry and it will never happen again.

Later that night mommy didn't go to work. She was in the room with daddy and they were making funny noises and its like they were wrestling, giggling and breathing hard.

The next day, mommy told me to not tell her nothing like that or she will ground me for the rest of my life. Eye said okay.

Days went by.....Months went by....and a few years went by and daddy was still coming in my room kissing and touching me. It was when Eye turned 11 and Eye had some red stuff coming out of my private part which eventually Eye found out that Eye had reached puberty. Daddy had told me that Eye have become a woman and that he was proud of me. My body was starting to feel differently and Eye started to gain some kind of figure.

Mommy and Daddy relationship was falling apart because all they did was argue everyday. One day mommy asked me who would Eye rather stay with, her or daddy? Eye told her that Eye would rather stay with her and Eye asked her where Daddy is going to live at. She told me that my daddy has another girlfriend somewhere else and that they are getting a divorce. Eye was so confused at the time where eye didn't know how to feel. Eye knew daddy loved me a lot and wondered why he was leaving me. Eye was also use to him coming in my room at night cuddling with me.

Eye remembered the last night my daddy was at our house before he moved out. He came into my room for the last time and told me that he would always love me even if he wasn't living here. Daddy

starting to hug and kiss me a lot like he have missing
me. This time Daddy did something different. He told me he wanted to
make me feel better and wanted me to remember how he felt.

Daddy pulled my pajama bottoms & my panties down. He
rubbed my private part and stuck his finger inside of me. Eye was in
shocked and didn't know how to feel. It hurt a lot, then it started to feel
good, then bad, then good again. He then ask me did Eye want to see
something of his. Before Eye could answer, he grabbed my hand and
put it on his private part. He pulled down his pants and help my hand
on his private part.

Minutes later, daddy got on top of me and tried to stick his
private part inside of me. It didn't go in at first, but after a while it went
in. Eye was screaming and was in so much pain, then the pain went
away eventually. Daddy told me that he loved me a lot and that's why
he decided to put a part of him in me. He told me to not tell anyone our
little secret and that this is something that we will only share together.

Now daddy has moved out and Eye am feeling kind of weird.
Mommy notice that Eye am acting differently and walking differently.
She tells everyone that Eye am changing because Eye am going
through my changes in puberty. She doesn't have any clue that daddy
went inside of me.

A month passed by and Eye haven't seen or talked to my daddy
at all and Eye am starting to miss him badly. Especially him touching
and going inside of me. Eye start to get this horny feeling inside of me.
It's like Eye need to be touched by a boy or some kind of man. It was
older guys in my neighborhood who use to just stare at me and flirt
with me, but eye never looked their way. Now Eye am starting to want
the attention from them all the time. Eye start sneaking boys in my
house and they would touch me like daddy use to touch me. A few of
them went inside of me with condoms on and some of the others didn't.
Eye don't know what is it, Eye wanted sex all the time. Eye loved the
feeling and it gave me so much comfort.

Years passed and now Eye am fifteen years old and in highschool. The last time Eye talked to my daddy was two years ago when Eye was thirteen. He was asking me questions and if Eye have told anyone our secret. It's like he put fear in me not to tell anyone, especially my mother. Eye wasn't comfortable with him touching me like he use to anymore because Eye learned that it wasn't right and Eye asked him why did he do that to me and lie to me about why he did it. My father just got mad and started arguing with me. To this day, Eye haven't heard from him.

My mother finally has a new boyfriend and he is living with us. He stares at me all the time and winks his eye at me often when my mother isn't around. One time he burst in the bathroom when Eye was getting out the shower and he stared at me before he left out and closed the door. One time, we was left alone in the house and he came into my room while Eye was taking a nap and started touching me. Eye was scared as hell and in shock, and Eye literally let him do what he wanted to do. Afterwards he threatened to tell my mom about the boys Eye sneak through my window at night if Eye told on him. My mother's boyfriend stayed in my room often. One time Eye tried to tell my mother that her boyfriend likes to stare at me all the time and she got so mad at me that she threatened to kick me out and to go live with my father if Eye speak on things like that again. It's like my mother was starting to get jealous of me or something, because guys will always compliment me on how Eye looked or dressed.

During these times, Eye have gotten so insecure about myself and was depressed all the time and felt that no one really cared for me. So Eye tried to fulfill those voids by having sex with random guys. It made me feel wanted. Eye then, started to hate myself afterwards. Eye hated the person that Eye have become. Eye had literally no one to talk to or open up to. All my friends were just worried about boys, fashion, and going to parties. One time Eye got date raped at one of those parties because we were drinking with some guys and they put something into my drink. All Eye know is that Eye woke up butt-naked in a guess room. No one even cared to ask me was Eye okay. My so-called friends left me alone at a strangers house and Eye basically had to catch a bus home.

For about two months straight Eye stopped going to parties and sneaking guys in my house because my mother's boyfriend wouldn't let me. It's like he wanted me to himself while my mother was sleeping. So Eye just played the game with him, why not, there was nothing else Eye could get comfort from.

Now Eye feel sick all the time in my stomach, and Eye am always tired and sleepy. Multiple times Eye have came to my mother, telling her that Eye don't feel good but all she tells me that there is nothing wrong with me and that Eye am just trying to get attention.

One day Eye was so sick that my mother had no choice but to take me to the hospital. When we got there they wanted to run some test on me to see what was wrong. So my mother and her boyfriend left me at the hospital and Eye had to spend the night.

Early that morning, my doctor came in and had a weird look on his face and said that he need to call my parents up here to hear the results. Now this had me kind of nervous and paranoid. After about a hour, my mother and her boyfriend arrived. They were all in my room and the doctor arrived. The doctor told them to sit down and he gave us the results........

The doctor said that Eye am seven weeks pregnant and that Eye have H.I.V.

My heart dropped and Eye started crying and screaming so hard that Eye had a panic attack. My mom yelled at me and asked me what boy Eye let, get me pregnant. Eye told her, it wasn't a boy, it was your boyfriend and he probably gave me aids too.

My mother's boyfriend started laughing and he told my mother that he always told her that Eye was crazy. My mother yelled at me again and told me to stop saying stuff like that and the reason you probably caught H.I.V., is because you are going around sleeping with everyone. After a long back and forth argument, my mother and her boyfriend left me in the hospital because the doctor wanted to keep me there another day.

At this moment, Eye was scared, pissed off, alone, and just tired of everything. What am Eye going to do with a baby.....and if my mother finds out that the baby is her boyfriends', then she will kill us both. Eye just had to get out of this hospital.

It was about ten at night and Eye decided to check myself out of the hospital. Eye got up, put on my clothes, grabbed my belongings and Eye was out the door. Eye knew my way around my city, so Eye went to the nearest bus stop. Before Eye got there, a strange man called me saying "hey lil mama, come holla at me." Me being stupid, Eye walked over to him and Eye saw some other guys in the alley as well. As soon as Eye walked close enough to the alley, the guy snatched me by the arm and through me down on the ground by the alley. Eye hit my head so hard against the ground, Eye didn't even scream. Eye was kind of dizzy.

All Eye can see and feel , is the guy pulling my pants down while the other guys was touching me all over. Eye just laid there and thought to myself that Eye am just tired. It seems as if Eye was dreaming because Eye didn't hear a thing but my own thoughts.

Then all of a sudden....POW!!!!

*In case you are wondering what happens next....there is no next. Eye was raped and shot in the head. Eye died instantly. Eye don't even know if Eye had a funeral or if anyone was there that actually cared. Everyone abused me mentally and physically. My only regret is that Eye should have told someone when my abuse first started. Eye should have reach out to everyone in my path. It's too late now, only my spirit can touch those who are able to share my story to other girls that may be going through what Eye went through. Eye wish Eye could have live longer than fifteen years old and experienced a real life of love, peace, and joy.*

This is happening not only in the Black Communities but in every community as well and is being swept under the rug. That's why most of our young sisters are so sexually active and is so out of control.. They are confused, afraid, insecure, sick, and they are using sex as a medicine to keep them calm. They are afraid and ashamed to speak upon this because they don't know how, and they are worried about the effect that it will have on them and their family, more like an embarrassment. These girls are being touched at a very young age and as they get older they tend to think it's normal. They start to like it and they don't innerstand why they do, but they continue to let their father, step father, and these Men continue to touch them.

This is why most of these women are so insecure and they only use their bodies to draw in attention from Men. You can feel their broken bodies when you hug them all the time and they will be very timid.

You can really tell who is a victim to this without them even saying anything. Their energy, actions, and eyes never lie. Eye have been around so many women who are victims. These women are never satisfied and it's impossible for them to be with one Man because they are too sexually disturbed to remain idle in a relationship. They get bored easily. They obtain these perverted demons from their molesters and different men that they have had sex with. They tend to be angry & so difficult at times for no reason at all.

Eye am so sorry that some of you women have went through this, but you must talk about it to someone that you love or trust. Holding these demons in, will only damage you more mentally, physically, and spiritually. Please, having all these random sex partners is not going to take that pain away and that empty void that you are feeling inside. Stop forcing love and affection. Learn how to exhale....release those demonic energies that hurt you. If not, then those same energies will only draw you to more men with similar demonic forces that you will be deceived by.

The sad thing about this is that some of their mothers don't even care or they don't want to believe that this has happened or is happening to their daughters. This is real life...this is happening as of now. Some of these women let these Men do this to their own children just to satisfy their men so he want leave.

So don't be quick to bash or judge these sexually active women out there, because they are sick....they are mentally disturbed and they need help. They don't know how to control their demons. But as they get older, they have a choice to get that help, but some don't, because they don't want the help. They choose to stay who they are. They are trying to kill themselves by thinking they can drink or smoke the pain away, including Sex. They are committing suicide and dying a slow painful death everyday.

Believe it or not...Eye believe that 65% of our women have

been molested growing up. Maybe more, and they won't say a word about it....They are so afraid.

Eye discussed this topic with women on social media of all ages and these were their responses:

**Goldyn Akachi**
A lot of people hide this inside because they
think they are alone and that no one else
has been thru this...

Your post about sexual demons really got to me because im sure ive been experiencing that for years now. I was molested alot as a child and for some reason i ended up sleepinf with alot of men trying to fill something inside of me. Its like i wanted to be in control of my sexuality. I wanted to be able to say no one forced me like they did when i was a child again. Ive only had 1 real relationship that was abusive & resultes in me having my son. My sona father is also not in the picture. Which makes me feel like i failed my child by not being able to provide him with a stable family foundation.

**Fifine Baker**
As a victim myself eye thank you **Goldyn
Akachi** for this post it means alot to me
some people just don't know how it is and
how it affects your everyday life because of
it and some of these people are your family
members

**Charlene Pirkle**
Damn that hurt my heart. The one thing my mom taught me was to never ever accept abuse of any sort. She took a lot of crap just to protect me. I'm crying thinking of someone not being protected. I live and breath for my children to keep thier innocence and self esteem. I'm so sorry for anyone whom is or has gone through this. You are precious. You are needed. Your voice and life and respect matters. Get away and tell someone asap. Find shelters or other love ones to stay with. If not in your city..research quickly and find shelter somewhere else but do it asap. Get help.

Lakira Hall
Very sad and true indeed, although this did take me back to a very painful childhood memory, it helps to talk about it.

**Raven Marie**
Almost cried

**Racquel Sylve**
I have also always believed that you can feel the brokenness when you hug, or come into contact with someone who's been hurt real bad 😞😞

**Char Bey**
This needed to be address and more need to speak out on it. Many of our people have taken on the behavior of the beast and need to be handled. smh

Anna Marie Fleming
Sad but true. They really need help not only the ladies but it's happening to our young men also.

**Triana Sadler**
Very sad and true and it happens so much I was molested by my bus driver as a young girl he would try to leave me so he could find me walking and lure me into his car,I hate buses and I can never look them in the eye for the fear it is him .Preachers always preaching about prosperity about what GOD gonna give you instead of healing the people and speakinh on real issues that matters

**Chrissy Shepard**
So true. I know a Pastor (demonic wolf in sheep's clothing) doing 70 years for rape and molestation. We need to somehow start another victims group for this. Who out there is with it? We are losing our children!

**Sonya Grace-Jones**
True and I am planning on writing a book about this because it happens more than we know. One of my old friends, my daughter's old friend. I never experienced this personally because I was a talker and they usually go after the quiet type. Very nice post. This is a warning, mother's watch your young ones and question everything.

**Chrissy Shepard**
I am so sorry for whatever happened to all victims. Every last one of you need to get it out. Otherwise it will eat you alive.
Remember, we have to start from the inside and work out way out. One could have and wear every designer outfit on the market and look beautiful. But what's going on inside.
Can we talk? This is a very serious problem.

**Brooklyn Garcia**
Thank you for all the wisdom and knowledge you share!!!! SO TRUE!!!

**Single Parenting & Teen Pregnancy:**
**(Removing the Betrayal, the Bitterness & addressing with the issues with Solutions.)**

Your one mindset & emotions from your heart shifts you away from living the life that you really desire. The moment that you shift your thoughts away from the lack of love and limitations that you set on yourself, you will see the positive, productive change come into your life."

There are a lot of men who are Emasculated, they are also known as Beta males because they don't love or respect women and they are horrible fathers. Guilty or Not, these Beta Males are not gonna stand up for you or help raise their children, so don't expect them to do anything without you forcing the issue.

Eye am not taking your side or the men side. Eye am on the Truth side and Eye see the reality of things How can any man love (RESPECT/HONOR) his woman when a lot of our women are single mothers? How can men say he loves(RESPECT/HONOR) his woman when he doesn't think she is not even good enough for him to be there to help raise his children.. How can the man say he loves(RESPECT ,HONOR) his woman when he only see her as a sex symbol and he only uses her for his personal pleasures? Eye can go on but Eye think you get the point. Some of these men do not even know how to build anymore within their own home, so they abandon their women and children?

Women...your gonna have to learn to stay strong and hold your own until these Emasculated, Beta Males wake up. All they do is talk, talk, talk, don't be deceived by words and no action. There are still some real Masculent, Alpha Men out here, but we can't do this alone. We cannot mentor every single child out there who has no father. We can only do so much within our area. Stop putting your trust in the fake men who screams for attention to create a false image, but rather trust and Respect that man who is building with you in your home or giving you the Real wisdom to love and protect yourself and children, until you encounter a real Man that will Love, Honor, Respect, & Protect you.

Your babies and children are not dolls. You have to teach them more than just knowing how to be cute. They must grow older and be taught right or they will continue the same cycle.

How did we come to a point where we think it's funny and cute to hear our little children curse and say bad grown up things? How did we come to a point where we think it's funny and cute to see our little children imitate sexual things that they see on t.v. or hear on the radio? How did we come to a point where we are letting our children dress so provocative & sexual while knowing that there are child molesters watching your children everyday? And some of you have the nerve to exploit your children on the internet. Then we have the nerve to act all shocked and mad when our little children end up pregnant or end up getting someone else pregnant. We have that stupid look on our faces like we don't even know why our children is out of control. Everything starts in the home, and if that home is unstable, then that child will walk with a lean, ya dig? An ignorant fool will only raise their children to become fools. You must teach your child in the way they should go. Teach them to be better than you, our future is in the hands of your children.

A life long connection born from temporary lust. The inncocent suffer when we go our separate ways. Broken homes seen to be the norm nowdays. This is not the way i wanted it or imagine it!!!!

We have to fix this? Can we learn from our bad decisions that we make in our life? Can we stop praising teenage girls and single women when they get pregnant by guys that don't even want them? So, is this the Norm now? No it isn't...and we should not accept this. We should not be teaching our kids this neither because we are only confusing them thinking it's the Norm to be raised by one parent or have multiple people that they call dad or mom. When are we going to take the time to sit and listen to our kids tell us how they truly feel about this. Eye converse with a lot of kids and trust me, they are confused as hell and this is why they are so quickly to get pregnant because they know that they are going to get the attention and praise. Once you bring a soul into this world, your wants are not first anymore.

YOU MAY NOT SEE A PROBLEM WITH THIS, BUT YOUR KIDS DO, & YOU WILL NEVER KNOW HOW THEY TRULY FEEL BECAUSE THEY KNOW HOW YOU REALLY ARE AND YOU DON'T EVEN TAKE THEM SERIOUS ENOUGH TO EVEN LISTEN TO THEM.

If you are a teenager and you have just found out you are pregnant, and will soon have a baby, it becomes a very difficult situation for all parties involved. It is important for everyone to realize that the pregnancy can be okay, as long as the decisions made are well thought out. The best thing to do, is to seek out all possible options, and then discuss them with someone who can help you. Whether you are about to become a teen parent, or you have a teenager who is pregnant, there are valuable coping methods you can practice that will help you through this time.

First, make sure that you are a hundred percent sure that you are pregnant by checking in your local clinic or doctor's office. Next, by telling your parents can be one of the hardest things about finding out that you are pregnant. It may be terrifying to not know what their reaction will be when they hear the news. Don't let this fear stop you from telling them. The sooner you let them know, the better. The best way to go about doing this it is to be direct and honest. Once you break the news, answer all of the questions they may have for you with honesty. Be prepared for mixed reactions. When you tell your parents the news, you will have to experience their fresh reactions of just finding out. If your parents have a negative reaction, remember that it will be okay. They may get angry or emotional at first, but with time, they will get better. Remember, they will be hearing this news for the first time, in front of you, and they do not get to prepare for how to handle their initial reactions. Just don't expect to get praised like others when they become pregnant. Some people react in different ways, especially if they are religious or if they prefer you to be married before having a baby.

Also, you have to build a support system. Tell your parents, family members, or your school's counselor for emotional support. It can be very difficult to share this type of information, but it is important to let someone close to you know immediately. No matter what decision you make about the future of your pregnancy, you should allow someone to help you through it. Please know who the father is and be sure that he knows and is involved. Don't feel like you have to handle the responsibilities of your pregnancy alone. It is important to involve the father and his parents, even if he doesn't want to. Whether or not you decide to move forward with the pregnancy, you can receive emotional, or financial help from the father. Make him step up and never have the mindset of not needing a father in your child's life.

Never try to hide your pregnancy from anyone because you will only make your situation worst. We all need one another at times. Me personally, Eye don't believe in abortions, but rather Eye believe that if a woman or teenage girl cannot take care of her baby or doesn't want it, then should should just give it up for adoption. Having abortions damages your body and once a life is created inside of you then it's not your decision or authority to take that life away.

A unplanned pregnancy can really make your life difficult at times. Becoming a mom when you're still young yourself is an incredibly tough choice. For girls who get pregnant in high school and the years right after, it's not always easy to tell what the next few months and years will look like, which is why Eye asked a 12 girls to get real and tell the truth about their experiences as teen moms. They talked about changing college plans, career paths, finances, relationships, friendships, and more. They also explained what they wished they had known before they got pregnant, and the struggles and challenges they've faced.

(Krystal- 19yrs old.) "I got pregnant just a few weeks before graduation, when I was 18. I wish I would have known that going to college was going to be almost impossible. It's not so much a financial thing as a babysitting issue. I don't want my son in daycare when he is so small. And without daycare, or someone to watch him, I don't have a way to go to school. I want to work but I also want to stay at home with him. I have to basically beg my son's father to help me out at times when he is not mad at me."

(Jada- 19yrs. old) "I was 18 and fresh out of high school and confused as hell. I thought I was so in love. One thing I wish I had known was how big of an emotional toll being in separate households from my boyfriend was going to be. It felt like I was a single mother and I developed terrible baby blues, which caused me to leave the father of my baby because he was out chasing other girls. Also he only came around just when he wanted to have sex with me. He didn;t really care about our baby."

(Brooke- 20yrs old) "I was 19 when my daughter was born. The one thing I wish I had known about being a teen mom is how much my life would change. Being a mother changes your life anyways—being young is just a bit more stressful because you haven't experienced much of life yourself. It's all a learning experience. I love it. I don't mind that I can't go out all the time and party like my friends my age do. But I do miss being able to just get up and go wherever I needed to. I can't do that anymore. I have a human to look after other than myself. You truly do give up your needs —not completely, but they're not in first place anymore!"

(Miracle- 16yrs old) "I just had my baby and the hardest part is worrying about how I'm going to support my kid financially. I have a lot right now, but I do need a lot more stuff for the baby. It's kind of a burden to put on my parents to help me provide for my baby when my boyfriend doesn't want to work."

(Jennifer- 23yrs old) "I got pregnant at 16 and had my baby at 17. I wish I had known how insanely hard it would be. Forget the screaming baby and the poop running up their back while you're trying to rinse spit-up out of your freshly curled hair. It's the amount of stress, the lack of support, and the stereotypes that comes with being a teen mom and trying to prove people wrong. Nobody wanted the mom with a baby at their girls night out."

(Ariana-20yrs old) "I found out I was pregnant for the first time right after I turned 18. I wish I knew how much I would have to give up for the well-being of my daughter. It wasn't until I had to decide between something for her or something for me that I realized that she was the most important person in my life. My needs and wants were no longer relevant. All that mattered was giving that little girl everything she could ever need and more."

(Stephanie- 23yrs old) "I was 19 when I had my son. I wasn't prepared for all the things that were going to change. My goals, aspirations, even my social life —everything slipped away from my norm. I wish I had known that I would lose so many relationships due to my child. Too many people who didn't plan on sticking around met my son, and some of them he happens to remember. Listening to him tell me how much he misses people who chose to exit his life is overwhelmingly heartbreaking."

(Haley- 23yrs old) "I was 17 when I got pregnant. I wish I knew how hard it would be to juggle everything. It's like I had to put my life on hold. My senior year in high-school was hard and deciding not to go to college at the time. It's tough to find a reliable babysitter so that I can work."

(Lisette- 29yrs old) "I was 15 with my first pregnancy and 16 with my second. The hardest part of being a young mother was the misconception and stigmatization from society. Adults are cruel and the lack of support from society puts you down and makes you feel ashamed of being a parent. I also felt that my children were being judged on the sole reason of having me as their parent. I wish I wouldn't have felt ashamed or embarrassed."

(Leah- 43 yrs old) "I was 16 when I got pregnant and 17 when my daughter Ari was born. I finished high school by taking college classes at the University of Minnesota. Guidance counselors helped me make that choice. I was raised by my parents with the expectation that I would go to college after high school, so I went to college about an hour's drive from home and I brought my baby to college with me. Balancing college classes, raising a toddler and having a social life was the hardest part of teen motherhood. I wish that I would have better

understood the impact that my day-to-day decisions had on my child —
choices like moving apartments a lot, leaving her with babysitters,
spending too much time away from her, and even the 'normal' mistakes
that teenagers make. When you have a child, you are making mistakes
for two, not just yourself and those mistakes will affect your kids
forever. But that struggle also shaped who I am today, and fostered my
desire to make the world a better place for all people who struggle in
life."

(Christina- 36yrs old) "When I found out I was pregnant at the end of
my sophomore year of high school, my life was derailing. I was
drinking and smoking pot and couldn't have cared less about school.
My GPA was a 0.05 and I have the transcript to prove it. When I found
out I was pregnant, I had a profound and sudden paradigm shift. I
realized my actions not only affected me, but that of the unborn child I
chose to keep. I pulled myself together, started going to class, and
making up credits. I ended up graduating on time with the rest of my
class with a 4.0. I went on to receive a B.A. and a Master's degree."

(Tianna-17yrs old) "I wish I would've never have gotten
pregnant. Don't get me wrong, I love my baby, but I wasn't thinking
about all the responsibilities that came with it. I was just having
careless sex. Well, to the girls out there that's having babies early, they
better be mature enough and ready to take on this huge responsibility.
This is no joke. The babies are cute but they can also send you through
a depression stage if your not strong minded."

To these sisters: In this life, you will never be given more than what
you can handle. Take one day at a time and put your child first, your
faith and effort will help you through anything. This lady told me that
she was a single mom at sixteen and it seemed like a distant dream to
her now. Her son is now 11, and day by day she made it through. It was
one of the most challenging experiences that she have ever been
through. She said this will make you a stronger person. I'm not saying
there won't be days that may seem impossible, or there will not be tears

shed. But if you have the fight, you will make it. That same woman is now 8 years married with 3 children and she still have days that seem unmanageable, and she still shed tears. It really helped to become involved with other positive people or women who are experiencing motherhood. They will become a second family to you. They will support you. You may make some life long connections with these people, and you may run into someone to be called your mentor. She may have been down the same road as you, and will help you out immensely! Just remember, you do the best you can with the situation handed to you, never beat yourself up.

Also Eye want to say to all you girls who are 14, 15, 16, or 17 and pregnant...... thank you for sticking with it and not having an abortion, that's amazing on all of your parts. You have so many other options and your baby will be a blessing. It will be tough, but more fun and love than you could have ever imagined. Just remember "Nobody said life would be easy, they just said it would be worth it"

## Overcoming & Dealing with the Pain of loosing a Mother & a Father......The Story of Anasis Fair:

Anasis Fair will never forget the day her world came crumbling down. How could she? It happened twice. When she was 13yrs old, her mom, Sandra, who had been her motivation, logic, inspiration, common sense, spiritual confidante and everything moms are to their daughters....died from pneumonia-like symptoms.

"I heard about death and people's parents dying, but I thought there was no way it would happen to me.", said Anasis, a senior at Houston's Aldine High at the time while on the basketball team.

She said her mom smoked and had a lot of fluids and she was too young to know what the exact cause was.

"It was unbelievable when my mom died. But I feel she's still here. I think of her everyday."

When Anasis' world crumbled, she didn't crumble with it. Instead, she picked up the pieces as best she could.

A year after her mother's death, Anasis would hurry from school to the side of her then-ailing father, Alvin. Loosing both of her parents by age 15 has not prevented her from standing strong.

She use to hurry to McDonald's where she worked at the time then would rush back to her father's side. Not only was he battling cancer, but he had diabetes. And Anasis wanted to make sure he got his insulin shots on time.

After she would leave her father, she'd go home, exhausted, for a few hours each night, then get up in the morning and start over again.

Home at this point, was with her older sister Tangie Brown, who had assumed custody of Anasis and their younger sister Angela, when her dad got sick.

"I wanted to work, so I could help my sister out," said Anasis, who had to share her small living quarters with both sisters and her Tangie's 3 kids.

"Whatever $90 or $100 I got, I gave to her. Or I took it to get some food for my dad. It wasn't much, but it was something.

Rather than to sulk in her own misery, Anasis has tried to be the woman that her mom was. When it seemed to be too much, Anasis found peace and a chance to escape on the basketball court. She began playing basketball at 14, the same year she moved in with her sister.

"There was a time, I wanted to give up," Anasis said. But when I started playing sports and being around people that makes me laugh, it started releasing some of the pressure I had."

That pressure reached an all time high when her dad died of cancer during her sophomore year in high-school. At 15 she had already lost both her parents.

"I thought my dad would always be here to walk me down the aisle and to be there for me," Anasis said. "And I thought my mom would be there just to support me. It hurt....and it still hurts."

"The reason I keep wanting to do better is because I look at the way my parents brought me and my sister up, and they tried to make sure we were better off than they were," Anasis said. "They did the best they knew how. We didn't have to have the best things in life. They always told us that somebody would always better. But as long as you're happy with the things you have, you can make do.

"And mom always stressed to me to finish school. At least make it through high-school. Every time I think I want to quit , I know that's not what they want me to do. I would disappoint them, and I would disappoint myself. I wouldn't want that."

Anasis would become the first high-school graduate in her family." And whatever Anasis needs, her mother and father provides for her in spirit with a peace of mind.

"I pray every night," Anasis says. "God doesn't put more on you that you can bear. I think of that. I could not have a house and things could be worst. I can't have all the things I want. The things I do have now have to satisfy me. It will workout in the end. There's a lot more ahead that's going to be pretty good."

## Suicidal Thoughts:
## (The decision)

## Poem By: Duneika Benjamin

"What the fuck do I have to live for? I feel like I am just in the way. I feel like I am an inconvenience to everybody. I feel like I am just taking up space. I try to talk to people about my problems but they will just tell me to pray. But I really want someone to love me, hug me, and to show me the way. You see, everyone thinks I am okay because I keep this smile on my face, but they don't know how many times I sit in my room and contemplate. Like, should I do this tonight? Or should I wait until 2day. To take my own life, because this life, I can't take. You see, I put that pistol to my temple, and I put that knife to my wrist, because I got so much bullshit on my mental, that I believe my death would be bliss. And what's sad is that I don't think my sorry ass would be missed. But I think to myself, do I really want to go out like this, and the answer is no. So I put down that pistol, and I put down that knife, because no pain, no stress, and no depression is ever worth me taking my life. So I continue to fight and give this life all that I have to give, because dying is too easy, so I challenge myself to live."

Dealing with the thoughts of suicide, we cannot look for a permanent response for a temporary problem that we have the will to overcome. We just have to really go within our inner strengths.

Honestly, this makes me sad because Eye truly care for my sisters and all our women out there. No, Eye don't know you at all. Eye might walked passed you, or caught a glimpse of you driving down the road, but chances are you live far away from me, in another state or even in another country. Eye love you all just the same. Even though we are distant, we are not so different, you and Eye.  Eye too have felt intense pain and felt like giving up. That was too easy for me. Eye think that everyone thinks about suicide, that's something that everyone thinks about at one time or another, if they're honest with themselves. Eye know that sometimes, pain can become so heavy to carry around that you might just think killing yourself is the only cure from how bad you feel. But don't do it. This is why.

Eye think what's happening to you is this. You are changing, both in body and mind. You are much like all other living beings. The caterpillar morphs into a butterfly. A crab searches for a new shell when it outgrows the old one. The old you, the one you're used to being, is dying. That's the one your loved ones know, the little girl who sat on their laps and listened to their stories, the one they tucked in at night and took care of when there was illness. They still see you as that person. Now, you're changing, right in front of them. You don't sound the same or act the same. Your likes and dislikes have changed. You used to give that cherry on top of your sundae to someone else. Now, you decide to eat that cherry yourself. Your family grieves for the person they once knew. All the stages of their grief — the anger, the denial, the guilt — are unfolding right before your eyes.

You are changing. Perhaps there is something about yourself that you are ashamed of in some way. Maybe you're gay, lesbian, or feel like you've been born in the wrong body. Or you might just feel like you are weird. Sometimes, especially in our teens, we feel disconnected, like we're watching things go on around us but we're not really a part of anything. Eye know because I've been lost before, many times. All those feelings, in part, come from shame. You were not born with shame, though, so you don't have to own it. It took years for you to learn that shame is a part of you, but it takes only a declaration from you to release it. You are what you are. Don't make excuses for yourself. Doing so only minimizes who you are now and who you will become someday.

If all this isn't enough, you also have to deal with bullies at school and a bunch of haters who come in all ages, races, occupations, and religions. Maybe you even find them in your house of worship. Some of these people think they have God on their side, as if He chooses one of His children over another. Yeah, it's crazy. If you think about it long enough, though, you can see how people come to believe what they believe, but it doesn't make them right any more than it makes you wrong. Don't take these people seriously. It will only bring you down.

Get used to the new person who is growing inside you. Look for support near and far. The Internet is full of people telling their stories on blogs and discussion threads. You are not alone. You will be amazed by how many people are like you. It's a great feeling when you make a connection to a total stranger. It's even greater when you realize what a help you have been to a stranger. Maybe together you can navigate this crazy world.

Yes, Eye love you. Eye want to give you a big hug and tell you that it gets better, because it actually does. Once you accept the person you are and forgive the ones who have wronged you, you will start to grow. Hang on. There are people you may not even know yet who are waiting for you with open arms, and they will love you unconditionally. Trust me. Your life will get better, and you will learn how to love again. Promise.

**Azira Gomez**

*"Who are you today? You won't make everyone happy. Know this, accept this and continue to be you."*

"Never give up on yourself
Never underestimate the power of making eye contact and smiling at a stranger. Many people feel Invisible in society quietly drowning in their own self afflicted prisons they haven't learned to get out of. Your acknowledgement can help save someone. Be one of the reasons why this world isn't so ugly, you never know who you are inspiring or saving."

*"Those who were Broken & Abuse are more powerful because we know how to survive. Our spirits are pure while we sit back and analyze the world. We are different...we see and feel things different than most. We evolve more and are always deep in thought into higher dimensions. You have to be born strong and be able to endure any pain or nothing Eye just said will matter or be true. This doesn't justify the weak."*
*-Goldyn Akachi*

# INTERLUDE: THE APPRECIATION OF A WOMAN'S WORTH

*"A Queen is wise. She has earned here serenity, not having had it bestowed on her but having passed her tests. She has suffered and grown more beautiful because of it. She has proved she can hold her kingdom together. She has become its vision. She cares deeply about something bigger than herself. She rules with authentic power.*
                                                          *-Marianne Williamson*

*"My first book "Freedom of the Mind, Is a Peace of Mind."*

*"They say, "Behind every strong Man is a strong woman."....but Eye say, "On side of every King, is his loyal Queen." She is the one who keeps the man balance. She lets him be a Man. She lets him learn from his mistakes. She tests the bricks while he is building. She adjusts his posture when he is leaning crooked or feeling fatigue from providing & protecting. Even with her body covered, sexiness, can't even describe the woman's essence, for that is an insult to her elegance."*

*-Goldyn Akachi*

*Chapter 8*
# TRUTH SYRUP

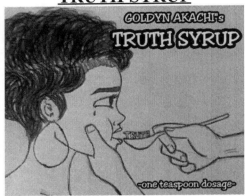

*"She is a butterfly in a hurricane, just trying to find her way home,*
*and I will always bet against the storm"*
*-JmStorm*

## 1st Dosage:
*"How can you love me or anyone, when you don't even love*
*yourself?...How can you be secure of our relationship or any kind of*
*relationship with anyone else, when you are so insecure with yourself?"*
*\*That is the question?*

## 2nd Dosage:
*"You're either going to GET BETTER or GET WORST....& you may*
*even get left behind. As you get older, your going to wonder where your*
*life went, and when you take a look at your surroundings, there will be*
*nothing but peasants around you. Maybe you are fooling yourself and*
*you are right where you want to be.....and that's nowhere!!! You suffer*
*from sloth & your own comfort."*

## 3rd Dosage:
*"Those who CAN'T, will always talk negative about those who CAN."*

## 4th Dosage:

*"Nothing Beautiful, asks for attention. Just because Eye don't react, doesn't mean Eye didn't notice."*

## 5th Dosage:

*"The craving you've been having inside is not actually sexual.....but it's a deep hunger for intimacy/closeness, that unexplained trust, and a spiritual connection."*

## 6th Dosage:

*"My sisters....don't let the only time you decide to act like a feminine woman be, when you are laying on your back with your legs open. A real Man prefers a gem and a delicate flower at times....not a hard rock."*

## 7th Dosage:

*"Sometimes holding on, does more damage than letting go."*

## 8th Dosage:

*"Any girl/female can be beautiful and attract boys...but it takes a Woman (Queen) to obtain knowledge & wisdom to attract Real Men/Kings."*
*\*What do you have to offer, besides your body? That is the question..*

## 9th Dosage:

*"You can't lose what you never had, you can't keep what's not yours, and you can't hold on to something that doesn't want to stay.*
*Also, You have to do what's right for you, no one else is walking in your shoes. You are your own obstacle, rise above yourself."*

## 10th Dosage:

*"Surround yourself with people that reflect who you want to be and how you want to feel. Energies are contagious."*

## 11th Dosage:

*"Pay Attention to those who care instead of trying to get the attention of those who don't."*

## 12th Dosage:

*"Women...if you are constantly using your body to attract Men, then you shouldn't complain when Men only want you for your body. So be very careful on what you are promoting about yourselves day in and day out. You are only tempting sexual demons."*

## 13th Dosage:

*"Ladies...If you are in a serious relationship or married. Eye know sometimes you may feel like your missing out on what's going on in the world, while you sit back and see all these other single women having fun going out and partying . It's normal to feel that way sometimes, so don't trip. Just remember....the grass on the other side it's not always greener. What you might be seeing is just an illusion because most of these single women would love to have what you have and be willing to trade places with you any day. They are still searching for that one person to slow them down so they can finally exhale because believe it or not, they are tired. So don't be deceived. What you have is value and most of the things you see in the world doesn't contain any value."*

## 14th Dosage:

*"It is better to be single than to end up trapped in the wrong relationship. If you don't have any clue on how to fix things when they*

*are broken, then it is best for you to not enter any kind of relationship."*

## 15th Dosage:
*"A silly woman girl looks at what a woman drives. A woman looks at what drives a man."*

## 16th Dosage:
*"You must gain morals to always know the difference between right and wrong, even when you see your parents going the wrong way."*

## 17th Dosage:
*"The worst kind of weight any woman can gain, is the weight of a weak man. Ladies, start holding these Men accountable for their actions. If you are leading this man and taking care of him...that's not your Man, but rather he is your child."*

## 18th Dosage:
*"Your not ugly because of the way you look, You're ugly because of the way you act."*

## 19th Dosage:
*"A woman's greatest cause of insecurity is when she starts to define her beauty within the media and within her peers. The question is...Who are you trying to look like or imitate?"*

## 20th Dosage:
*"You have been consumed by Media Indoctrination. You are no longer human. From birth you are a mindless, brainwashed drone waiting for your next programming like a junkie for a fix. You are a Corporate Bitch and your government is corporation's little whore...Wake Up!!"*

*Chapter 9*
# <u>"Becoming Self-Sufficient & Defining Your Own Destiny"</u>

CARRY YOUR SELF WITH CLASS,, NEVER TRASHY..
OUR IMAGE IS THE FIRST THEY SEE.. SO ALWAYS PUT YOUR BEST IMAGE ON.. PEOPLE TREAT YOU HOW THEY PERCIEVE YOU TO BE!

NEVER SETTLE FOR LESS , WHEN YOU DON'T HAVE TOO, MAKE THEM STEP UP,, NEVER TURN DOWN FOR ATTENTION !

RESPECT YOURSELF AND IT WILL DRAW RESPECT BACK!

LOVE YOU FIRST AND IT WILL DRAW LOVE TO YOU!

*"The greatest thing in the world is to know how to belong to oneself."*
*-Michel de Montaigne*

**Teen Self-sufficiency:**

You may have heard of the saying of being an Independent woman. Well what Eye am about to talk about is kinda similar to it but not all the way. Eye am not telling you to go through life thinking that you don't need a Man and that you can live life satisfied by not ever experiencing a real relationship because you are so in love with your success. Eye am telling you that you have to learn and be able to take care of yourself if you end up having to survive on your own. It's okay to depend on your man or spouse at times but you must be able to have his back when he falls, and he will. Most of all, you have to be able to have your own back as well.

Being self-sufficient can start for you around high-school, maybe early than that for some. During school, Eye know that boys love to buy you gifts or give you money just to show you how much money they have. If your not old enough to get a job, try to save some of that money that these buys give to you. Try not to spend it all at once. Even if you get a little allowance at home....put some to the side and let it build up. If you have any talents that you know of that you think you can make money off doing, do it. A lot of girls that Eye see that knows how to do hair at a young age are making money, and that's good. That's a very good step of being self-sufficient. You don't want to get to a point where you are running to your parents for money all the time. If you act like a child, then they will continue to treat you like one. The more you show them how responsible and self-sufficient you are, the more they will trust you and treat you as a mature young lady who can hold her own.

Boys know when you are in need of something because they will throw it in your face every time. They will show it off to you, but you cannot be a puppet for money. Don't put yourself in a position where you are dating boys just because you are in need of money. That is not a good look and it will eventually come back on you through your other relationships.

Okay, here are some tips and advice that Eye can give you to practice on being self-sufficient. Set Boundaries for yourself and follow your own rules...Discipline yourself. Establish firm rules and expectations that fit your family's lifestyle and values. For example, if you come from a single parent home and see that your mom or dad needs help to start dinner before you head out with your friends for the evening, help them. Make it understood that you want to help and that you feel that it is your responsibility too. This will also teach you how to be able to cook and feed yourself when you decide to live on your own or go to college, etc,etc.

Be generous at times at home or wherever you find yourself at most of the time. If you have any talents or ideas of making any job easier or just by offering your help, do it. This will benefit you and the person that you are helping, especially your parents. You will learn what hard work really means and you will hold value to the things that you put effort in creating and building. Those things last longer in life and you will be proud.

As a teenager you have no shortage of opinions. So use your mature opinions in family discussions respectfully. Thinking of turning the garage into a new family room? Give any other ideas about how you can gain more living space in your existing home? Teens want to be treated like grown-ups, so make yourself available to join them in the adult world when at all possible, and take the time to hear them out when they do have suggestions or concerns that involve the family or your home. You might be surprised at what they think of your great ideas.

Stay connected with all forms of communication. Teenagers like to be self-sufficient and want us to believe that they have everything under control—parents and adults know this, but that doesn't mean that they will stop keeping the lines of communication open and flowing. So when you ask questions, try to formulate them so that they require more than a yes or no answer. For instance, instead of asking how work is going, ask what they are actually doing at their job.

Texting is a great way to stay connected throughout the day. If your mom or dad has a busy day at work or after work, send a quick message "Eye hope you have a great day and I look forward to hearing all about it tonight." This shows that you care and think of others rather than yourself. Try to keep a journal of your thoughts and ideas and at the end of each week try to discuss it with your parents or someone close to you.

Always be supportive during any conflict and try not to throw temper tantrums. Always try to put yourself in your parents shoes and try to see things from their side. Remember, you are still their child. Criticize constructively, no one likes to be told they didn't do something right, particularly if it is done in anger. Choose how you criticize wisely. If someone fails a test or anything, don't say something sarcastic like "Well, if you had studied for this test instead of texting your friends all night long, this never would've happened." Instead, use a concerned tone and say, "It looks like you had some trouble with that test. How about if we set up a quiet time to study this week before the next test?" And try never to criticize in front of others; that never helps in this kind of situation. This helps you grow mentally and makes you become more mature.

Most of us have dreams for ourselves even before we become teens, but just because all the women in the family have gone to nursing school doesn't mean you have to as well. If you have an obvious interest or talent, despite the fact that it isn't something near and dear to your heart, learn more about your passion about it and encourage yourself every step of the way. When your parents or others around you see that you have set your heart on something, then they will encourage you every step of the way. You will tend to feel more comfortable and confident as well as being secure into your decision making. All of this mentioned above will help you grow into a self-sufficient adult woman.

**Self-Sufficiency as a Woman:**

The only reason you should be in a relationship is because you're in love. Keeping him around just because you no longer live with your parents and want someone else to take care of you isn't an excuse —you can take care of yourself. You don't need to know how to build a fire or rewire your house, but you should know the basics of surviving in the modern world. You don't want to always rely on a man to do everything for you, because you should be able to do them all on your own if it ever comes to it. That way you won't feel so depressed, empty, and helpless without someone.

When you find the man you want to marry, you'll probably pool your money together. There's nothing wrong with using his cash, as long as you know you could pay the rent for your apartment on your own if you needed to. You never know if your relationship will fall apart, and if it does, you want to be capable of living on your own. You don't want to be one of those women depending on the government or child support to take care of you for the rest of your life.

If you own a car, you should be able to change a tire and check the oil. You should also know where you keep your registration and what all of the lights on your dashboard mean. If you don't drive, you should have another form of transportation that doesn't involve your man, like taking the bus or the train. You have to be able to get around on your own, especially if you have an emergency and you don't have time to wait for someone to come get you.

None of us want to climb on a chair to murder the creepy spiders that cling to our walls. However, you shouldn't wake your man up so he'll do the job. You should be able to take care of your own house, whether that means dusting, vacuuming, or bug killing. Keep your house clean. They say that cleanness is next to Godliness. Take pride in where you live.

Making money isn't the only way to keep yourself out of debt. You also need to know how to balance a checkbook and pay your taxes. While you could always hire a professional to help you out or rely on your boyfriend to do it for you, it's always better to learn the skills yourself.

This is something that most women do not like doing anymore. With the rise of fast food and restaurants....no one wants to sit at home and cook anymore, everyone is too busy now. You don't have to become a five-star chef. You don't even need to learn how to use the stove. Just buy a few cans of food that you can heat up in the microwave, so you don't have to eat fast food seven days a week. But eventually your going to have to learn how to cook. A way to a Man's heart is through his stomach. Men love women who can cook like their mama. You don't even have to be just like mama, but at least prepare good meals. Sometimes you may get lucky by finding a Man that loves to cook but what are you going to do when that man is no longer around?

You don't want to be forced to call a repairman every single time you need to plunge a toilet or change a light bulb. That's why you should learn how to do simple repairs. You don't want to end up wasting more money than necessary, or waiting a full day until your man comes home to get the job done.

If you're one of the lucky ones that end up with a house of their own, you need to care for the outside as well as the inside. That means you need to learn to mow the lawn, tend the garden, and pull weeds. Your man shouldn't be the only one getting his hands dirty. Some Men think it is sexy for a woman to be handy.

Even if you're horrible with directions, you should know how to get to your mother's house, your doctor's office, and the nearest hospital. If your phone stops working and you don't have a GPS to rely on, you want to be able to get to your location safely. So pay attention while you are riding with your man or with friends. That way you will remember the streets and freeways that's around your area.

When you're in a committed relationship, you should consult your man before making any major decisions that concern him. However, you don't need his help to figure out what to wear or should you eat cereal for breakfast. He can't make every little minor decision for you. That's up to you. Learn how to think for yourself because one day you will have to teach your kids the same thing.

(From an Elevated Woman's point of view)

Being a single mom, Eye had no choice to become self-sufficient, especially while raising my Sun alone. An independent woman chooses to do things alone while saying she doesn't need a man, but a self-sufficient woman does what she can until the right Man comes along to help. Eye know Eye can't teach him everything about being a Man, but Eye can show him what a woman expects from a Man. Eye can also teach him that a foolish woman pays more attention to what a Man drives, but a good woman looks at what drives a Man.

His crown may be a little tilted, and his back maybe a little crooked while standing. But the one thing that Eye taught him is how to get up....even when he falls back down and regardless of how he wobbles when walking, he will have the heart to stand. Eye also teach him to become a protector, and how to provide for himself and the ones he love. Eye teach him the value of a woman and the value of a Man.

While he stands and walk through his journey, Eye remind him daily to always pay attention to the real Men that he encounters because Eye tell him all the time that he has to research and hunt for those missing pieces that Eye cannot give him. Eye have giving him a self-sufficiency technique.

So to my brothers and real Men....when you run into our Sons/Suns, can you please straighten up his posture and crown for me? He will be the one with good manners, making eye contact, and will always respond to you as Yes sir or No sir.

The most feared woman in America right now is THE SELF SUFFICIENT BLACK WOMAN! Who exactly is afraid of her? Well none other than the INSUFFICIENT BLACK MALES! So what does he do? He seeks to discredit her by attributing her strengths and his weaknesses to some made up Willie Lynch theory while deeming her independent and out of control. She's referred to as everything ranging from a Feminist to a Lesbian and all because she did what most of our parents taught us to which was to become successful. She's accused of wanting to control the black male when all she really wants it to be respected for her hustle, her struggle, and her achievement. Being self-sufficient woman does not mean that you are in competition with men or that you don't need men. This is just preparing yourself to be able to stand on your two feet and to have something to fall back on if you are left with your children. This keeps you from submitting to weak men that are no good for you.

**Defining Your Destiny:**

Self Encouragement of self-belief: The first step for leadership roles begins from within. You need to believe that the sky is the limit and not put a cap on your professional ambition. You should believe in yourself, take charge of your destiny and trust in your own capabilities to effectively manage responsibilities at work and at home with ease.

Make intentional career choices: You need to be intentional about your careers by setting standards of professional credibility to attract mentors. You need to define what is important to you and chart out your own path for success by actively speaking up and seeking help from people within your surroundings.

Create a self defined success path: Women leaders need to create an environment where they can define success and meet their ambitions not just within organizations, but also for communities around them.

Follow a "3R approach": To develop the leadership pipeline for women follow a "3R approach"— right roles, right client and the right sponsor. These factors should work in unison and should be developed equally.

Stay curious and open to opportunities: Leadership is often thrust upon a person when they least expect it. When it comes knocking, you should be ready to venture out of their comfort zone and grab the opportunity regardless of their apprehensions. You need to continue learning and stay relevant, while staying rooted in your vision.

*"How many of you set savings goals, career goals & health goals? How many of your friends/family know about them? How many are going to hold you accountable? Who are you going to hold accountable?? You are the company you keep. If you are the smartest, most stable, healthiest person in your circle, CHANGE YA CIRCLE!"*

**-Nesha Jenkins**
*(Bachelors & Masters Degree)*

*"Definitions belong to the definer.....not the defined."*
-Toni Morrison

While defining your destiny, you have to believe in yourself and you have to have the desire to want something in life. You know, fulfilling a purpose or a dream that you may have. If you want to know where your future is heading, just look at your friends and the people that you hang out with often. If you don't like the direction of where they are going, then make a detour. Do what you know that is best for you.

In high-school, you may have gotten to a point where you are tired of school. That's normal to feel that way but you must know that every little bit of education counts. Being a woman, you will need education if you want to achieve in the fields of your career such as being a doctor, lawyer, or even a business owner. How can you make the money you want if you are not knowledgeable of how to handle it. So with the free education that you get in high-school, please soak as much as you can.

Some say college is not for everyone and that's true, but if you have the chance to go, go for it. These days college is very easy to get into with all the grants and scholarships going around. You always want to get as much education that you can rather you like it or not.

If you have any talents or gifts....try not to do it for free for the rest of your life. That may be apart of your destiny to make that a career out of. A lot of people make great livings off their talents and the gifts they have. Some even become millionaires. Never be afraid to make that jump. Don't go through life wishing, "What If". You see, you will never know unless you try. Never be afraid to fail, because you will fall many times. The only problem with falling or failing is when you decide to stay there and give up. The choice is yours to define the path to where you are deciding to go. It even may change up along the way but never let anyone tell you that you are not good enough...smart enough...or don't have enough experience to achieve what you want.

*Chapter 10*

# "GOSSIP....SEPERATING YOUR NEEDS FROM WANTS"

*"Now days, most females are just running after what they want instead of just walking to what they really need. By running, it is causing them to keep bumping into one another that causes a competitive race."*

*-Goldyn Akachi*

Need- something you have to have
Want -something you would like to have

The difference between a need and a want is pretty simple until you set yourself loose in a store. Double chocolate chip ice cream? It's a food, so mark it as a need. That designer dress that fits you perfectly? Well, you need more dresses, so why shouldn't it count, too? Women love to shop, so please don't have the mindset that you need things before going into the store because you will end up spending way more than what you planned to.

*Defining Needs*
In actuality, you only need four things to survive:
   •A roof over your head
   •Enough food and water to maintain your health

•Basic health care and hygiene products
•Clothing (just what you need to remain comfortable and appropriately dressed)

Everything that goes beyond this – a big house, name-brand clothes, fancy foods and drinks, a new car – is a want.
Does that mean that you should only buy the things that you need? Not at all. Life is meant to be lived, not survived. Treat yourself to some wants along the way, but do so when you can afford to, and enjoy those wants as the extras that they are.

*Appreciate What You Have*
Once you become better at understanding the difference between wants and needs, you'll probably see that you've been able to fulfill more of your wants over the years than you realized. And that can be a major turning point.

When there are things that you want to buy or do that you can't currently afford, it becomes all too easy to focus on those things to the point of overlooking all the many things that you do have. Don't trick yourself into feeling deprived when you aren't. Take time to reflect on all the ways that you've been blessed. Then, decide what's really important to you, and go after it. So many people talk about wanting to do this or that, but they never actually try to make it happen. Be the person who makes it happen. Come up with a plan, and act on it. Even if it takes you a really long time, just working towards a goal is empowering. It makes you feel capable, instead of deprived; it makes it easier to tune out all those things you don't need, and it puts you in charge of your where you'll go next.

Being a female, you guys are the biggest victim of having so many wants. Especially when your girlfriends loves to gossip about the hottest trend. They say things like "Girl I need that, and I will die if I don't have it." Note that, this is only a trend of a false need because after this trend is over and the next trend approaches, then you will realize that you really didn't need those overpriced shoes or purse after all. You cannot get caught up in a needy world because it will drive you crazy. You will end up doing anything to get what you so-called need. These are wants and desires, that's all. A lot of us want to eat sweets and junk food all day but in all reality, eating that all the time will makes us sick. So, we have to keep a balance in our wants and to know when to not consider our wants a need.

Eye have been talking to a lot of women and Eye have come up with some things that the average woman truly needs while living her life's journey:

**Sex.** Research shows that having an active sex life reduces depression and anxiety. Additionally, having sex increases self-esteem, reduces stress, increases quality of sleep, and boosts one's overall immune system. Furthermore, when you reach orgasm, oxytocin (the bonding hormone) is released, and an amnesic effect takes over which can last for up to five hours. This doesn't mean that you need to go have sex with any and everybody. This is for those who are in serious relationships or married, not teenagers.

**Sleep.** Yes, you need lots of sleep. Never work yourself too hard or stay up every night partying so hard that you don't have time to get a good night's rest. You need your beauty rest. Maybe this is why some women are always cranky with an attitude. Coffee doesn't replace sleep. Don't fall into the gossip of women saying that they are too busy grinding to sleep or the only people that sleep are broke people. That's foolishness. Your health is your true riches.

**Exercise.** Here's the deal: exercise is Miracle Grow for the brain. Regular, aerobic exercise remodels our brains for peak performance by decreasing stress, lifting your mood, and sharpening your intellect. Overall, it simply helps you function better as a person. Yoga is great for your mind, body, and soul. Every female should learn this. Don't believe the gossipers when they tell you to just accept what you are and be beautiful. The key is to be beautiful and healthy at the same time.

**Connective Relationships.** We are all social animals and we crave positive, connective relationships. A healthy relationship helps increase one's confidence and ability to grow as a resilient person. So, if you've finally entered a healthy, loving, stable relationship, that experience can shift the brain's old negative beliefs allowing for a tangible shift in your core self. This is a need....so by you wanting to hang around those negative, messy people for entertainment purposes...that is only destroying you mentally and stopping your personal growth.

**Stimulating Mental Activity.** Just as exercise and sleep are building blocks for your brain, so is stimulating the mind. Whether it's via work or creative hobbies, using your mind to meet specific goal driven tasks not only helps the fibers of your brain to connect in a deeper way, but it helps you feel accomplished as a human being.

**Play Time.** Children are not the only ones who need play time — adults need play time too! When was the last time you got so lost in the moment that nothing else mattered? Allowing yourself time to be creative and spontaneous and soak in new and innovative experiences is essential to the human spirit and gives one a sense of balance in life.

**Physical Touch.** Eye am not talking about sex. Eye am talking about a hug, a caring squeeze of the arm, a holding of the hand. We are born with the need to be touched. If a baby or child is not held or cuddled enough, he or she will not thrive. A warm, safe touch releases oxytocin (the bonding hormone) as well as reduces levels of the stress hormone, cortisol . In effect, the body interprets a supportive touch as someone saying "Eye am here for you."

**Community.** There's a reason for the old saying, "It takes a village." Like children, we all need a village or in other words a community, which helps us to feel a part of; a sense of belonging. We are all social animals, hence our value of self is strengthened by the support of a team, a tribe, a village, a group, etc. Being a part of a community via shared interests (i.e. work, church, synagogue, sports, a club, etc.) is what brings the most meaning to our lives.

**Recharge Time.** Just like a battery needs to recharge, so do you in the most simple non-stimulating ways. This is just the time to relax your mind like watching goofy shows that you normally don't watch or playing video games, etc,etc. Mindless, winding down time is just as essential for your well being as anything else. Remember, it's all about moderation and balance.

**An Observing Ego.** This means taking the time to understand and observe you. It amazes me the amount of people I see walking around completely disconnected from themselves emotionally, physically and mentally. Without a connection to you, living your life in a satisfying way is impossible.

How can you learn what your growing needs are without truly understanding you? How can you learn to trust your instincts and make decisions without reflecting on what drives your behaviors? Learning to comfortably observe your own steps in the world is one of the most invaluable gifts you can give yourself and there is no better time than now. Once you learn your true needs, then you will be able to balance your wants and to not let them control you.

# "THE OUTRO"

This book was not created to cause division between the Man and the Woman, but rather to go inside of the woman's mind to repair what is broken so we can rebuild that connection back between us. Eye also have a book for us Men as well called "In2 The Mind Of An Elevating Man". That will also repair what is broken within us so we can rebuild our connection with you even better.

Classy is when you have a lot to say but choose to remain silent in front of fools.

*"Dedicated to every elevating woman in the world."*

Made in the USA
Columbia, SC
09 April 2023

14618665R10076